China's Brave New World

and Other Tales for Global Times

JEFFREY N. WASSERSTROM

Foreword by Vladimir Tismaneanu

Indiana University Press
BLOOMINGTON AND INDIANAPOLIS

This book is a publication of

Indiana University Press
601 North Morton Street
Bloomington, IN 47404-3797 USA

http://iupress.indiana.edu

Telephone orders   800-842-6796
Fax orders   812-855-7931
Orders by e-mail   iuporder@indiana.edu

The paper used in this publication meets the minimum requirements
of American National Standard for Information Sciences—
Permanence of Paper for Printed Library Materials, ANSI Z39.48-
1984.

Manufactured in the United States of America

Library of Congress Cataloging-in-Publication Data

Wasserstrom, Jeffrey N.
China's brave new world : and other tales for global times / Jeffrey N.
Wasserstrom ; foreword by Vladimir Tismaneanu.
       p. cm.
    Includes bibliographical references and index.
    ISBN 978-0-253-34889-0 (cloth : alk. paper)—ISBN 978-0-253-
21908-4 (pbk. : alk. paper)
     1. China—Civilization—1976–2002.   2. China—Civilization-
2002– 3. Civilization, Modern—1950– I. Title. II. Title: And
other tales for global times.
    DS779.23.W38 2007
    951.06—dc22
       2006035028

2 3 4 5 12 11 10 09 08 07

CHINA'S BRAVE NEW WORLD

This book is dedicated to Anne, Sam, and Gina, who listened to and commented on the earliest versions of all of these tales.

And to the editors at newspapers and magazines I've worked with in recent years, who patiently taught a sometimes difficult pupil important lessons about writing that he hadn't learned in graduate school.

Contents

Foreword: Beyond Marx, Lenin, and Mao

Jeffrey Wasserstrom is not only an insightful historian, but also an active public intellectual. The essays collected in this volume propose a very personal, provocative, erudite, and morally compelling approach to China's ongoing "Great Transformation." I'm not a China expert, but I read them with enormous interest. What Wasserstrom does is show us how the old mythologies, long cherished by Chinese communists, have become increasingly obsolete.

True, much of the old system is still there, at least at the symbolic level. Institutionally, the Communist Party still exerts full control. For all the thousands of internet cafés, Starbucks, and modern bookstores, there is still a scarcity of open debate on the country's recent past. Discussing Mao's real biography or assessing the Cultural Revolution remains taboo. Some of the recent Western writings on Mao may be exaggerated, but it is hard to separate him from some of the worst human rights abuses of the past century. In one of the best essays, Wasserstrom imagines what Mao's reactions would be were he to come back to life and witness the immense changes, especially in the economy, social structure (the rise of the new bourgeoisie, encouraged by the party/state), and culture. I agree that much would terrify and outrage the once-worshipped "Great Helmsman." Still, as Wasserstrom correctly points out, he would be happy that the country is still run by the Leninist (or, more accurately, Maoist) party, and that ideology, exhausted as it is, still enjoys an unquestioned monopoly. Or, better said, whenever someone questions this monopoly, the person suffers immediately the consequences, including marginalization, harassment, imprisonment, or expulsion (depending on how serious the transgression is deemed by the regime). Market Leninism, as some authors describe contemporary China, is based on the attempt to reconcile ideology-driven authoritarianism with the restoration and cultivation of private property. For Lenin and Mao, no doubt, such a mixture would have been the ultimate apostasy.

For years, East European dissidents have focused on changes in the People's Republic of China. For people like Adam Michnik, Jacek Kuron, Vaclav Havel, and Miklos Haraszti, China has always mattered. The Tiananmen protests, and the June 4th Massacre that crushed them, were major parts of the series of events that resulted in the breakdown of communism in East-Central Europe. Wasserstrom explains the nature of the Chinese upheaval of 1989 and shows that Western media tended to focus on certain visible symbols, ignoring or downplaying the complexities of the story. The Goddess of Democracy was more than an expression of admiration for American-style democracy. Workers, as much as students, were involved in the movement.

This is a lucidly optimistic book. Wasserstrom has studied the East European transitions and realizes how important the role of critical intellectuals was in developing civil society initiatives. The most successful transitions occurred in countries where such intellectuals and civil societies managed to act decisively. On the other hand, nationalism was also a corrosive force, and Wasserstrom's discussion of the many faces of Chinese nationalism is truly illuminating.

How peaceful will be China's exit from authoritarianism? Can we expect this to happen in the near future? Can modernity be reduced to technological progress? How long can the appeals of freedom be suppressed? Wasserstrom's book comes out at the right moment: fifty years ago, in October–November 1956, the Hungarian intellectuals, many former convinced Marxists, led a popular uprising in favor of pluralism and freedom. The revolution was crushed by Soviet tanks. Mao was among those who most intensely and decisively pushed Nikita Khrushchev to organize the military action against the Hungarian legal government and its supporters. Half a century later, Hungary is a free country, and the statues of the former leaders have been amassed in a special park that Wasserstrom describes with wry irony. Reading this book, we can anticipate that one day such a park may well exist in Beijing or Shanghai.

Vladimir Tismaneanu
Washington, D.C.
May 10, 2006

Introduction

Questions about China's recent past and future prospects are currently high on the agenda of intellectually curious members of the American reading public, one of the main audiences for which this book is intended. They are also of steadily growing interest to others who may be drawn to a work with the phrase "tales for global times" in its title, such as instructors who teach and students who take classes in international studies. And questions about the People's Republic of China (PRC) are likely to loom larger still in the coming months and years, thanks to the media frenzy sure to accompany the lead-up to and staging of two mega-events. One of these events is, of course, the 2008 Beijing Olympics, already the subject of intense debate (over whether holding the Games in China is justified, given the regime's human rights record) and speculation (over such things as how many medals PRC athletes will win and how Zhang Yimou, the acclaimed director, will choreograph the opening ceremonies).

The other upcoming mega-event, which has so far generated mostly excitement and interest inside the PRC but will get more global attention soon, is the 2010 Shanghai World Expo. At least according to its promoters, this "Economic Olympics" will be the first World's Fair held in a developing country and will bring tens of millions of visitors to Shanghai. Hopes run high that it will give the city the sort of boost that London got from the Crystal Palace Exhibition of 1851 and Paris got from the 1889 Universal Exposition for which the Eiffel Tower was built. And the boost that Chicago got from the 1893 Columbian Exhibition that introduced the world to the Ferris wheel—making it no accident that one thing Shanghai is doing to

In the back are the Peace Hotel (built in 1929) and, to its right, the Bank of China (built 1937), while in front is a sculpture celebrating Beijing's successful bid to host the 2008 Olympic Games. *Photograph by the author, taken in Shanghai.*

prepare for its World's Fair is building the tallest Ferris wheel of all time.

"How has the PRC changed since the death of Mao Zedong (1893–1976)?" "Will China soon stop being one of those few hold-out countries (Vietnam, Cuba, and North Korea are the others) that continues to be governed by a Communist Party in this post–Berlin Wall and supposedly post-Communist era?" "When I take my first trip to China"—and in the minds of many of this book's imagined readers, the question is typically now phrased as a "when," not an "if" one, unless they have already gone—"what kinds of things do I need to know that I am unlikely to learn from the mainstream media?" "And how accurate or distorted is the image of the PRC that is typically conveyed when American television shows or news magazines focus on the country?" Inquiring minds, as the old ad for the *National Enquirer* tabloid put it, want to know. The chapters that follow are designed to help them satisfy their curiosity.

The answers to the Big Questions I provide, though, as readers will soon discover, tend to be offered in a roundabout rather than a direct manner, and to be given via engagement with more fanciful sorts of questions of my own devising. For example, to provide a sense of how China has changed during the last three decades, I ask what Mao Zedong, if magically brought back to life, would make of the streets and stores of contemporary Nanjing. And to show that, where China is concerned, globalization does not simply equal cultural homogenization with American characteristics, I ask: does it mean the same thing when a Starbucks or a bowling alley opens in Beijing as opposed to Boise, the Canton in China as opposed to the Canton in Ohio? (Short answer: it does not mean the same thing to bowl a strike or order a latte in the two Cantons, and it can even mean quite different things to do these things in different Chinese cities, due to regional variation and contrasting local histories.)

Too often, Americans curious about China feel they have only two options: accept the overly simplistic answers to big questions provided by a soundbite-driven mass media, or look for alternatives in stuffy academic works that can be off-putting due to the style in which they are written. I want to offer a third option: a playful look at serious issues, provided by a scholar who devotes his working life to teaching and writing about China, travels regularly to Asia (ten trips in the last twenty years, ranging in length from eleven months to less than eleven days), and is concerned with how people, objects, ideas, fashions, and modes of popular culture flow across borders. The result is this collection of short pieces, which some might call "essays" but I prefer to label "tales." This is because most include arguments and some even have a thesis or two, but all rely heavily on vignettes, observations of things seen while in transit, and stories.

Questions about the PRC are not the only ones that are now high up on the agenda of my imagined readers (yourself included, or you would have stopped reading by now), nor the only ones that I address. Another set of Big Questions that I grapple with and fancifully recast in the tales to come relates to globalization. This book strives to provide illumination concerning this over-used and oft-abused term, which only made its way into newspapers and magazines in the 1960s, but by the end of the century had become impossible to avoid.* In doing so, I focus on one globalization question too seldom asked in the debates on the subject (except, perhaps, when historians like myself are the center of them): How exactly are the current flows of people, ideas, and products across borders similar to and different from flows of this sort a century or two ago?

In confronting this question, as in confronting the Big Questions about China, I strive to offer an alternative to both soundbites that strip complex situations of their complexity and scholarly writings that seem unnecessarily obtuse, at least to the uninitiated. And with questions about globalization, as with questions about China, my working assumption is that striving for illumination and indulging in playful speculation need not be incompatible. Hence the coming chapters try to tease out similarities and differences between global flows and global cities of the past and present through the discussion of everything from Jules Verne novels to a short story fragment by Liang Qichao, one of the leading intellectuals from the closing years

---

* And there is no sign that the popularity of "globalization" as a buzz word is on the decline, as shown via the admittedly statistically flawed metric of a Google search for the term I carried out on April 13, 2006. The result: 121 million hits in .05 seconds.

of the Qing Dynasty (1644–1911), to a twenty-first-century comment on Shanghai by Italian designer Giorgio Armani.

Before giving some more clues (or, rather, teasers) concerning the ways that the tales in this book approach questions about the PRC and globalization (and of course the manner in which China is contributing to and being reshaped by global flows), I want to do something that historians like to do whenever given the chance, even in a book that is largely concerned with the most contemporary of issues: look backward. In later chapters, I look back a century or two at times, but right now, I don't want to look back very far at all. Just to 1982 (when I set off to Harvard to work on a master's degree in East Asian studies), 1984 (when I transferred to Berkeley to enter a doctoral program in history), and 1986 (when I took the first of my eight trips to China—the other two Asia journeys that bring the total up to ten, for those keeping track, were to Taiwan).

The main thing I want to stress about 1982, 1984, and 1986 is simple: China did not then loom nearly as large in the American imagination as it does today, nor was it routinely seen as a key player in global flows of people, goods, money, fashion, and ideas. Magazines such as *Time* and *Newsweek* would occasionally devote a feature story or even a special issue to China, but not with the regularity that they now do. It seemed unthinkable in 1986 that twenty years later a citizen of the PRC would be presenting an Oscar at the Academy Awards, as Zhang Ziyi did in March 2006. It would have seemed improbable then that I would ever walk into a U.S. post office and have my eye caught by the image of another citizen of the PRC, basketball star Yao Ming, standing tall as the dominant figure on a poster showing NBA stars, but that is just what happened to me recently. And when I started graduate school, the thought that I would have to (or get to) go to China multiple times struck people as a novelty: circa 1982, even in highly educated circles and in moneyed circles, a day-trip into the PRC from the then–Crown Colony of Hong Kong was all that most people had done or thought they were likely to do.

There has often been curiosity about China in the United States (a theme returned to in several chapters) and there was some then. It was not fueled by fears of economic competition, interest in Chinese films, or any number of other things that currently fuel it. But it was there. Americans were starting to find it easier to visit the PRC, and even if only a tiny percentage contemplated seriously taking a trip there, this did increase curiosity.

In addition, ever since Nixon met Mao, links between Beijing and Washington had been growing stronger. And there was fascination in the early 1980s with Mao's successor, Deng Xiaoping (1904–1997), who had been dubbed "Man of the Year" by *Time* back in 1978 (and would win the title a second time in 1985) and made a celebrated trip to the United States in 1979. Back in that pre-Gorbachev era, Deng was lauded as the first Communist Party leader who seemed capable of speaking a political and economic language that the West could understand. And back before he played a key role in the June 4th Massacre of 1989, which put an end to the student-led protests that centered around Tiananmen Square, he was routinely treated by the press as the kindest and gentlest Chinese Communist Party (CCP) leader with whom we had any right to expect we would ever have to deal. But even before the massacre, these positive images were paired with negative images (such as the imposition of the then-new one-child family birth control policy) that aroused curiosity.

Still, while there was undeniably some interest in China twenty years ago, Japan was the East Asian country that was attracting the most attention. It was Japan, not China, that was the rising economic star of the region. And it was Japan, not China, that was the country that inspired the most admiration and the most hostility, the strange mixture of excitement and fear that the PRC is now drawing. If I had told people back then that I was studying Japanese history, they might well have been surprised that I was concerned with Japan's past rather than its present, but they took it for granted that Americans needed to know more about the Japanese "miracle" and maybe even Japanese culture. To mention that I was doing graduate work on China, by contrast, tended to be a conversation-stopper at parties, in a way that it is not for the students I now help to train.

It seems worth stressing, before moving on to describe the structure of the book and the nature of some of the chapters to come, that the tales I will tell of two decades spent occasionally traveling between the United States and the PRC and almost that long teaching and writing about China for a living are stories situated in a period when American interest in the PRC has been on the rise. They are also tales that speak to an era that, as I will show later, is not the first one of its kind, when China has alternately inspired, scared, and confused ordinary Americans.

The PRC of late has also, it is important to remember, been a country that has continually confounded the predictions of experts, myself included. Many of us were surprised by the size to which the Tiananmen protests of 1989 grew, the brutality with which they were suppressed, or both of these things. (For my part, it was the former much more than the latter that caught me unaware.) And we have been surprised by the ability of growth rates in the PRC to stay so high for so long. Aware of this, and of the long tendency for Western understanding of China to be distorted by fantasies and fears, this book generally eschews predictions. It nevertheless tries to speak to a time (the present moment) when there is a widespread desire to get a clearer idea of a land that both baffles Americans and seems ever more important to the American as well as the global future.

With these aims now laid on the table, let me return to questions in order to give a sense of how the book will unfold. Not the big ones about China and globalization asked and then often answered in wonderfully simple but misleading ways by purveyors of soundbites, but the less expected ones that lie at the heart of the tales I want to tell. Here are some of them. Why did posters showing Mickey Mouse with a stake driven through his heart appear on the streets of a Chinese city in the 1980s? Despite the hoopla surrounding the centenary of George Orwell's birth, could it be that one of his Eton teachers, Aldous Huxley, wrote a novel even more useful than *1984* for making sense of post-Tiananmen China—and, perhaps, post-9/11 America? Which famous Chinese historical event inspired both a Charlton Heston movie and an episode of *Buffy the Vampire Slayer*? And why, after the Berlin Wall fell, did some Hungarians decide that state socialist monuments should be theme-parked rather than destroyed?

These are just some of the curious questions asked or answered in the pages that follow. They are brought up in tales that touch in passing on many cities (European and American as well as Asian) and on literary works as disparate as Jules Verne's *Tribulations of a Chinese Gentleman,* Chinese globetrotter Li Gui's *A New Account of a Trip Around the Globe,* and Emily Hahn's *Times and Places*—a work that poses its own share of unusual questions, such as: Wouldn't Marco Polo's relatives have grown bored of hearing their famous kinsman go on and on about Asia's wonders?

Even though the chapters that follow are geographically and topically diverse, there are several unifying threads that tie them together. Most notably, all have something to do with China and draw upon the reading I have done about, classes I have taught concerning, and trips I have taken to the country. There are Chinese connections even in chapters that seem at first to have nothing to do with China. For example, one purpose of the visit to Hungary that inspired my tale of Budapest, "Karl Gets a New Cap," was my mission to deliver posters from Maoist times (1949–1976) to that city for use in a local exhibition. And it was interest in China that led to my fascination with Emily Hahn, the subject of another chapter, who lived in Shanghai in the 1930s and is best known now as the author of *The Soong Sisters.*

Another unifying thread is a concern with how new forms of entertainment, new patterns of communication, and new trends relating to consumption have altered—or left unchanged—our experience of living in and traveling through a shrinking world, and why a sense of place still matters in an era of runaway globalization. This is why certain products (such as Big Macs), settings (such as theme parks), and forms of mass media (such as television) show up in multiple tales. Above all, though, what unifies the chapters to come is that each tries to raise doubts about some form of conventional wisdom regarding China (for example, the notion that the Tiananmen protests were basically the same, aside from the way they ended, as the demonstrations of the same year that broke out in Eastern and Central Europe—there were, in fact, many differences that were overlooked at the time and now are too often forgotten) or globalization (for example, *pace* Thomas Friedman, the notion that a "Big Mac is a Big Mac is a Big Mac"—this is not true, as what seems to be the same burger can mean radically different things in different settings).

A final common thread is a tendency, wherever possible, to try to strike a light tone, even when dealing with issues and events of considerable seriousness, such as the resurgence of Chinese nationalism, a phenomenon that I witnessed up close when I happened to be in the PRC just when NATO bombs hit China's Belgrade embassy. The book as a whole is offered up as a kind of antidote to a sound-bite sensibility that thinks even the most complex questions can be answered simply. But it is also a brief for the ideas that those who wish to combat such a sensibility should not limit themselves to writing in ways that can be off-putting or impenetrable to all but a handful of specialists and that adopting a style that leaves no place for moments of levity may be counter-productive.

Turning to structure, the short pieces to come are divided into four parts, each made up of a quartet of chapters. These are followed by an afterword that looks at, among other things, the state of play of the ongoing love-hate relationship between China and the United States.

Part 1, "Adventures in China-Watching," is comprised of reflections and stories inspired by trips to East Asia—the PRC in the first three chapters, Taiwan in the fourth. The inclusion of that final chapter may seem odd or controversial, given the extent to which Taiwan has functioned for decades and continues to function as a country quite separate from the PRC politically, and given the intensity with which many residents of the island claim a distinctive Taiwanese identity. Yet, it fits for several reasons. The political name for Taiwan is still Republic of China (ROC), which has the word "China" in it. My impressions of the island have been, as I note in the chapter, shaped a great deal by immersion in Chinese history and the time that I spent in the PRC before first setting foot in Taiwan in 2004. And, finally, despite the relatively unchanging political relationship between the two countries, the flow of people, goods, and money between the PRC and ROC have increased dramatically—to the point where an estimated half-a-million citizens of the latter now work and reside in Shanghai.

In part 2, "The Inscrutable West," I turn my gaze toward the United States and Europe—though always keeping China in the corner of my eye. The first and third chapters focus largely on two cities, St. Louis and Philadelphia, that would seem to have nothing to do with China, but are linked to that country, in my accounts, via travelers who moved between these American urban centers and Shanghai. Part 2's second chapter, "Traveling with Twain," teases out similarities and differences between the trip to Europe that became the subject of Samuel Clemens' first best-seller, *Innocents Abroad*, and the way twenty-first-century Americans experience journeys to that part of the world. I also note in it that, though Twain never made it to China, he was very interested in it in the 1860s, the decade when he wrote *Innocents Abroad*, and later in his career wrote about Chinese political events and the treatment of Chinese immigrants to the United States from time to time. "The Time Machine of Tippecanoe County," the tale with a Twain-like title that ends part 2, looks at an Indiana heritage festival and returns to themes addressed in many of the preceding chapters: the ways that members of different cultural groups understand and misunderstand one another, how ideas about the past shape contemporary events, and the novel ways that history is being packaged and consumed in varied places, including China and the United States.

Part 3, "Turn-of-the-Century Flashbacks," explores the mood in different parts of the world at specific moments around the time when the last millennium gave way to the current one. Three of the chapters were inspired by experiences I had abroad. But one chapter, "Patriotism in Public Life: The United States in 2001," was inspired by staying in the United States during the months following 9/11, yet feeling for a time as though I were in a foreign country (one that was like the PRC in certain disconcerting ways).

Closing out the main body of the book is part 4, "The Tomorrowland Diaries," a quartet of chapters made up of ruminations on the future. "China's Brave New World" revisits George Orwell and Aldous Huxley's best known books. "Chicago in an Age of Illusions" asks how the theme-parking of one of America's leading urban centers may be a portent of things to come. Following these two chapters is "Why Go Anywhere?" It brings a new continent into the mix, using a visit to Australia as the jumping-off point for a series of musings on how travel can continue to involve so many encounters with the unexpected—even if one is an American spending time in a foreign locale that some insist has become thoroughly Americanized. "Faster than a Speeding Bullet Train" looks at old and new images of and futuristic fantasies about Shanghai.

Closing out the book is "Rhymes for Our Times," an afterword that revisits and extends themes addressed throughout the preceding chapters. One of the issues it takes up is the ongoing tendency of Americans to project onto the world's most populous country positive and negative fantasies that reveal more about our own hopes and anxieties than they do about people living across the Pacific. Being wary of this tendency is crucial at the current moment, I suggest, as dreams of the China market and nightmares of the China threat yet again gain strange and powerful currency in the United States as well as other lands.

PART ONE
ADVENTURES IN
CHINA-WATCHING

In the foreground, Xintiandi (New Heaven and Earth), a trendy Shanghai shopping and entertainment district known for buildings that, while recently constructed, follow a local architectural style popularized in the early 1900s. *Photograph by the author.*

1. Burgers, Beepers, and Bowling Alleys

Coverage of Chinese events late in the last century and early in this one has continually demonstrated that the American media's strange love-hate relationship with the PRC remains alive and well. Now, as in the early- to mid-1900s, we see shifts between periods when China is presented as a big, bad place that poses a threat to all we hold dear and periods when it is presented as a land of decent people on the verge of converting to our ways and buying our products in record numbers—just as soon as they overcome the lingering hold of a few outmoded traditions. There are some novel aspects of the current situation. The old spectres of the "Yellow Peril" and "Red Menace" have disappeared from the rhetoric of demonizers, for example, replaced by new visions of things to worry about on the economic and military fronts—worries symbolized by cover stories in U.S. magazines such as "The China Price," which claimed that its title was made up of the "three scariest words in U.S. industry" (*BusinessWeek,* December 6, 2004), and Robert D. Kaplan's "How We Would Fight China," which predicts that the PRC will prove a "more formidable adversary than Russia ever was" (*Atlantic Monthly*, June 2005). Similarly, there have been changes over time among those promoting the Americanization line, with recent favorite motifs including photos of NBA star Yao Ming and reports of Chinese people going bowling, buying stocks, and eating Big Macs. The general pattern—that goes back to the days of Fu Manchu movies and of Pearl Buck novels detailing the lives of yeoman Chinese farmers—remains surprisingly constant, but there is one key difference: swings between demonization and romanticization, which used to take place over the course of years or even decades, have begun to occur much more quickly of late.

For example, in the spring of 1997, with the Hong Kong handover looming and books such as Richard Bernstein and H. Ross Munro's *The Coming Conflict with China* making headlines, demonization was in vogue. By October of that year, however, thanks to the smoothness of the handover and plans by China's paramount leader, Jiang Zemin, to privatize the economy, the Americanization myth was back in fashion. A still-faster turnaround took place on the day in 1998 when President Clinton reviewed the troops at Tiananmen and then held a televised joint press conference with Jiang. In its lead-up to the first event, the American media trotted out every possible variation on the big, bad China theme. By the time the press conference ended, however, the burgers-and-bowling theme was again the order of the day. Since then, the burgers-and-bowling imagery has remained strong. But there have been slides back toward demonization. One of these occurred in 1999, thanks in part to a series of anti-American demonstrations and the crackdown on Falun Gong launched by the CCP. Another, flagged by the just-mentioned *BusinessWeek* and *Atlantic* stories, began in 2004.

Even when the Americanization narrative has been in vogue lately, as has often been the case, some commentators have continued to work in brief asides about Beijing's severe limitation on freedom of religion in Tibet and other things that people in the United States identify with the CCP's problematic human rights record. The main thrust of much recent coverage of China in the United States, though, has been that the PRC is becoming Americanized— not just Westernized, but Americanized. The media continually measure the economic and cultural distance the Chinese have come in recent years in specifically American terms—the number of KFC franchises or Starbucks outlets per city, for example. The political distance China still has to travel is also being measured in a similar fashion: it is common to hear American reporters asked about the prospects of democracy taking hold say that some trends are positive, but that we should probably not expect to see national presidential campaigns in China anytime soon.

Back in 1998, in a Beijing speech, Clinton claimed that one reason he made the trip was to help Americans get a "full and balanced picture of modern China." It is true that—thanks in part to the speed with which images of demonization and Americanization have given way to one another—the coverage began to *feel* considerably less one-sided around the time of that speech than had often been the case in earlier periods. Unfortunately, juxtaposing contrasting images of a generically despotic and rapidly Americanizing place—as occurred so dramatically during that Clinton visit and has re-occurred at various points since, including around the time of George W. Bush's trips to the PRC—does not provide a "full and balanced" picture of anything.

One general problem is that we end up hearing very little about things that do not fit easily into either story line. For example, we get occasional comments from demonizers about women being coerced into having abortions, and those entranced by the Americanization myth sometimes describe a day in the life of a female yuppie. Nevertheless, we seldom hear any serious discussion of the complex ways that economic reforms have been affecting Chinese women, for better and worse. It is not just that assessments of the positive or negative aspects of the Chinese scene are exaggerated, but that there are too many silences on major issues.

In addition, both the demonization and Americanization myths foster misunderstandings of specific things going on in the PRC. Consider, for example, the damage done by the burgers-and-bowling fantasy. This imagery obscures the extent to which China is being influenced by many foreign cultures, not just America's; karaoke bars are more numerous than bowling alleys in Shanghai, for example, and sushi is as popular as Starbucks. The Americanization narrative also distorts our understanding of Chinese ideals and practices.

This kind of distortion certainly happened back in 1989—a classic moment when the Americanization myth was dominant. Captivated by the media's focus on students quoting Tom Paine and rallying around an icon reminiscent of the Statue of Liberty, Americans often failed to realize that many of those who took to the streets were workers angered by official corruption and their inability to form independent unions—not the absence of elections.

The American media also failed to grasp or to effectively convey that the student activists themselves were inspired as much by patriotism as by foreign ideals. They wanted to get the Chinese Revolution back on track, not derail it, to make China strong on its own terms, not Americanize it. Just as the Americanization myth obscured the fact that the "Goddess of Democracy" was a complex symbol with Chinese as well as foreign referents, it obscured the influence of non-American struggles ranging from South Korean student protests to South African hunger strikes and the extent to which nationalistic and democratic desires intertwined at Tiananmen Square.

Yes, students quoted from "We Shall Overcome" and other American protest songs. But the song they sang the most at some points in the struggle was "Children of the Dragon," a work suffused with patriotic imagery that was written by Hou Dejian, a singer who emigrated from Taiwan to the mainland in the 1980s and then was forced to return to the place of his birth due to his active support for the Tiananmen protests.

What problems are there with the more recent image of China as a land of burgers and bowling? One is that there are hundreds of millions of villagers who have never seen the Golden Arches or tried to roll a strike. There are also many migrant workers living in ramshackle urban squatters' camps who would not dream of dining at a nearby McDonald's; such a splurge would cost them many days' wages.

The burgers-and-bowling imagery also leads to a distorted understanding of the experiences of even those young professionals whose life stories enter the U.S. media. This is because even the most seemingly "global" or "universal" symbols can end up meaning very different things in different places. One should never assume that buying a stock or watching a Disney cartoon has the same significance in China as in the United States.

This point came home to me with reference to Mickey Mouse (known in China as Mi Laoshu) during my first stay in China, which lasted from August 1986 until July 1987. Watching Disney cartoons on television was a regular once-a-week ritual in Shanghai back then, both for foreigners (starved for any familiar sort of entertainment) and Chinese urbanites of all ages (starved for entertainment variety, something in short supply in China then). Everyone in the city knew Mickey's name and what he looked like, and soon variations on his image were showing up in many different contexts. Advertisements for products that had nothing to do with the Walt Disney Corporation, for example. And, even more surprisingly, posters used in a public health campaign. Mickey's fame, plus the fact that the "laoshu" in his Chinese name can be translated as either "rat" or "mouse," made it natural that when an official effort to eliminate vermin was launched, some local artists began showing him being stabbed through the heart with a stake and being subjected to other violent fates that the creator of cartoons such as *Steamboat Willie* never imagined his best-known character suffering.

That globalization isn't wiping out all cultural specificity was brought home to me again in the late 1990s by a brief conversation I had, in England, with a young lawyer from Shanghai. He was complaining that he missed the nightlife in his home city and found London's a bit boring, an idea that intrigued me, given my experiences in Shanghai a decade earlier, and made me want to find out just what it was he did for fun. Remembering a big billboard for a new bowling alley that I had seen in Shanghai in 1996, I asked him if that was a place he missed. When he scoffed at the idea, I assumed I had offended him by suggesting that a refined, cosmopolitan person would engage in what many Americans still think of as a déclassé sport. His next comment showed how wrong I was: "Bowling," he said, "is for girls."

Many other apparent symbols of "Americanization" can be dissected in similar fashion. Take cell phones and beepers. In the late

A Shanghai street scene. *Photograph by the author.*

1990s, some dissidents would carry beepers so that sympathizers within the state-security apparatus could warn them when a crackdown was planned. Or consider the features of the Shanghai stock market that make it so different from New York's. One of its main functions is to help the government raise money to support state-run industries, and its stocks are divided into two classes, one of which can only be purchased by foreigners. In addition, though it is often cited as symbolic of China's increasing interest in connecting with the outside world, the Shanghai stock market's development has a good deal to do with the rising tide of both nationalism and localism in the PRC. It was allowed to expand before 1997 as part of a general effort by the national regime to ensure that when the handover took place, colonialist Hong Kong would not seem by far the most modern of Chinese cities. Another thing aiding the Shanghai boom was the increasing prominence in the Politburo of political figures with ties to that city. Some of these officials were delighted to see Shanghai surpass Canton as a trading hub and reassert its status as China's leading metropolis.

No survey of symbols of Americanization would be complete, finally, without a consideration of McDonald's—the corporation whose supposedly homogenizing power has led to the coining of the term "McDonaldization," a dystopian equivalent to McLuhan's rosier imagery of the "global village." Surely it means something that McDonald's gained a foothold near Tiananmen early in the 1990s.

It certainly does, but just what it means for McDonald's to be entrenched in China (and vice versa: in the United States, Mulan dolls were given away with "Happy Meals" when the Disney film came out and Sichuan dipping sauce has been offered with McNuggets at times to provide a "taste of the East") is a very complicated matter. Curious about the Americanization myth, I visited one of the then-new McDonald's in Beijing in the mid-1990s, and I was struck by an atmosphere quite different from that of a typical American outlet. Just how it was different was hard to tell from a single visit, and I was not interested enough to go back a second time.*

---

* An admission: on that trip, the restaurant whose bizarre meaning as a transnational symbol I spent more time pondering was a flashy Beijing eatery called "Auntie Yuan's Chinese Cooking from New York."

Luckily, a year after that trip, I came across the then-just-published but now classic *Golden Arches East: McDonald's in East Asia.* Edited by Harvard anthropologist James L. Watson, it was a treasure trove of interesting detail on the diverse ways that Big Macs are consumed and viewed in China, Japan, South Korea, and Taiwan. One value of the book was that it highlighted the intraregional contrasts that marked the way McDonald's became part of the culinary, economic, and social landscape of different East Asian cities. In doing so, it demonstrated just how misguided it is to speak generically of "Asian values," "Asian traditions," indeed, "Asian" anything.

The excellent chapter on Beijing by UCLA ethnographer Yunxiang Yan also showed just how often decidedly non-American meanings and practices had become associated with McDonald's in the PRC. I learned from Yan that Big Macs were viewed as part of a "stylish foreign cuisine" in Beijing, yet classified as bread snacks that happened to contain a bit of meat, as opposed to meat-based main courses. Yan also informed his readers that Beijing McDonald's restaurants were often seen by young couples of the early- to mid-1990s as romantic dining spots, and that families sometimes went there to mark special occasions in a relatively formal setting, as opposed to ducking in for casual getaways when too tired to cook, as in the United States. Yan described the development of novel customs such as the employment of personal greeters—nicknamed "Aunt McDonald"—who establish long-term relationships with young customers. He showed as well how the large number of one-child families affected everything from marketing to the handling of in-store birthday parties.

Essays such as Yan's—now being brought to the attention of new readers via the publication of an updated second edition of Watson's volume, which arrives, interestingly, after some U.S. franchises of McDonald's have made efforts to seem less impersonal, warmer places—move us closer to getting a "full and balanced" picture of China than do a score of magazine articles that speak in a very general way about how Chinese lifestyles are changing. It is based on close observation of the creative process by which real people react to new products and practices and put localized spins on transnational phenomena. Yan asks questions about eating at McDonald's that could be (but all too rarely are) posed about other activities, from protesting to surfing the web. How do Chinese of different generations treat Big Macs, he asks, and do men and women view imported fast food differently? Does income level matter? What is the impact on familial customs, as well as diet, of a new type of restaurant?

To be fair to the U.S. media, there are some very good China correspondents (more and more each year, in fact) who like to ask and answer these sorts of questions, and occasionally pieces that do this make it into print or onto the air. All too often, however, such pieces are axed or their impact is minimized by a flood of reports that ask only "How bad is China?" or "How soon will the Chinese become like us?" And it does not help that the books on Chinese themes that gain the widest readership in the United States often intentionally or unintentionally breathe new life into old stereotypes, rather than open American minds to thinking about China in new ways.*

In the end, thanks to their failure to make room for complexity, the demonization and Americanization myths, which seem opposites, turn out to have much in common. This is deeply troubling, especially because misleading imagery can and does affect government policies as well as the popular imagination. The Chinese deserve better. And a changing China—where burgers are for lovers,

---

* This has certainly been the case recently. Oprah Winfrey's September 2004 selection of *The Good Earth* as a reading for her book club meant millions were exposed for the first time to (or reminded of) Pearl Buck's vision of the Chinese people, which fits in comfortably with the Americanization narrative. And a year later, to shore up the demonization narrative came *Mao: The Unknown Story,* a biography by Jung Chang and Jon Halliday that presents Chairman Mao as a devil incarnate, a sort of Fu Manchu with totalitarian characteristics responsible for more deaths than Hitler, and which apparently gained a favored place on George W. Bush's bedside table. Newspaper and magazine reviews by those without any expertise relating to China have tended to praise the Mao biography, sometimes lavishly. Most specialist reviewers, though, have questioned just how much of the story told in the book is "unknown," been disturbed by its sensationalistic tone, and expressed skepticism about some of its claims (such as that there was nothing heroic about any part of the Long March) and frustration with the selective way that the authors use sources. My review, "Mao as Monster" (*Chicago Tribune,* November 6, 2005) was thus not unusual—though I seem to be the only specialist so far to have said it reads less like a biography than like a Dracula novel.

democracy is for nationalists, beepers are for dissidents, Mickey is a rat, and bowling is for girls—is just too interesting a place to be viewed as a mirror-image-in-the-making or the worst nightmare of a foreign land.

2. Mr. Mao Ringtones

For more than a quarter of a century, Chairman Mao's body has been on display in Beijing (a city whose name means "northern capital"), lying in a glass coffin that has always reminded me of the one in which Snow White's sleeping body rested while she awaited her prince. Perhaps because of this, I have sometimes found myself pondering what Mao would make of today's China if he were suddenly brought back to life (though just whose kiss would have that life-restoring power in this updated version of the fairy tale is something I have never sorted out). I suspect that the Chairman would have profoundly mixed emotions about the country he found upon awakening. On the one hand, he would be pleased to discover that the Communist Party was still in control of the country; that some taxis had images of his face hanging from their inside rearview mirrors; and that workers still sometimes carried his portrait through the streets. On the other hand, he would be dismayed to learn that the Party welcomes capitalists into its ranks; that, due to the spread of fast food franchises, many Chinese children are more familiar with the face of Colonel Sanders than that of any current political leader; and that when workers carry his picture these days, it is often to protest being laid off from jobs at state-run factories that were supposed to be theirs for life. He would be gratified that one can still sometimes hear "The East Is Red," the song comparing Mao to the sun that was heard constantly during the heyday of his personality cult. But the one place you do not hear this song less so these days in China is in flea markets, where peddlers of Mao memorabilia can be found trying to sell cigarette lighters that emit this famous tune (and a flame) when the top is flipped up.

My most memorable daydream about a revived Mao's take on twenty-first-century China came to me during a brief 2002 stopover in Nanjing, once home to the Ming Dynasty emperors (its name means "southern capital") and now the site of their tombs and the mausoleum of Sun Yat-sen (though no corpses of former rulers are on display here). The daydream began while I was sipping a cappuccino in one of the city's nicest new cafés, the walls of which are covered with giant black-and-white images of European landmarks, part of an effort to give a cosmopolitan ambience to a coffeehouse that (according to my waitress) was bankrolled partly by Taiwanese investors. I found myself slipping into a reverie wondering what Mao would make of this place (fittingly called the New Café) that is so completely unlike anything I encountered on my first trip to Nanjing sixteen years earlier, when suddenly something surreal happened. I heard the familiar strains of "The East Is Red" coming from the next table, but when I turned to look for the source of the music, the melody stopped, and all I saw was a man and a woman, no tape deck, no CD player. Then I noticed the man was talking on his cell phone, and the penny dropped: it had been programmed to play a "Mr. Mao song"—to borrow a phrase I once heard a Hong Kong hawker of communist kitsch use to describe tunes such as "The East Is Red"—whenever its owner had an incoming call.

That café would not be the only Nanjing establishment that would give Mao pause if he came back to life. Other sites that would perplex him include the city's luxury hotels (there was only one in 1986 when I first visited Nanjing, but now there are several), its elegant department stores (multi-story complexes of the sort only found in Hong Kong two decades ago), and its internet cafés (where young people can venture into cyberspace in search of world news or, more often, online entertainment).

If I could quiz Mao about his reaction to just one Nanjing site, though, it would be none of these. Instead, it would be the Xianfeng Bookstore or, rather, the various branches of this establishment (there were two when I went to Nanjing in 2002, three by the time I returned next in 2004). One of these—the original Xianfeng—is located very close to Nanjing University and is viewed by intellectuals in the city as a key center of literary and cultural activity, a fact demonstrated by the decision of *Nanda Wenxuebao* (Nanjing University cultural news) to devote a whole issue to the virtues of the place. According to one of the articles in this publication (free copies of which are distributed to patrons), it opened in 1996 as a small store (just 17 square meters in size) that catered to students and professors who wanted to buy or special order hard-to-find novels, collections of poetry, or academic texts. Within a few years, it had a large stock of books (about 30,000 in all) and a computer database to keep track of them all. It also has a significant number of loyal patrons. Some of these contributed essays to that special issue of *Nanda Wenxuebao,* in which they wrote quite eloquently about how important trips to Xianfeng to buy books or take part in special events (discussion groups, visits by famous authors, and so on) had become to them.

The second branch of the bookstore to open is considerably smaller (about half the size) and is located in an underground shopping complex near one of the sleekest of the new department stores. It does not host as many special events and it lacks the tables for drinking tea and coffee that can be found at the original Xianfeng. It does, however, have one advantage over its counterpart in the university district: an elegant curving glass-fronted façade. It also, at least when I visited it in 2002 and 2004, had more eye-catching displays, in the form of colorful stacks of books artfully placed about the store.

The Chairman would approve of the name of this bookstore: one translation of *xianfeng* is "vanguard," as in "Party leaders serve as the vanguard of the Revolution." It might be less pleasing to him,

The Nanjing University district branch of Xianfeng Books. *Photograph by the author.*

though, to realize that the proprietor had a second meaning of *xian-feng* in mind as well: "avant-garde," as in those who experiment with artistic forms. And Mao might find disturbing the obsession with bilingual labeling in each of the two branches that I have visited (and I assume in the third one as well). Both are known not just as Xianfeng but also as Librairie Avant-Garde, and French as well as Chinese subject headings show up on each shelf (Lishi/Histoire, for example). And even more disconcerting to Mao would be the first sights he encountered upon walking into either branch. In the smaller branch when I visited it in 2002, for example, one of the artfully arranged displays was made up of stacks of the Chinese translations of the three controversial Hite Reports on sexuality in America. To enter the original Xianfeng store that year, meanwhile, you had to pass by a wall containing images of Che Guevara (Mao might approve), Jesus Christ (Mao would be annoyed), and Marlon Brando and Al Pacino dressed for their roles in *The Godfather* (Mao would just be mystified).

Browsing the stacks, the Chairman would find a wide variety of works—much more diverse in terms of authors and topics than he would expect to see, and much more diverse than a Western visitor whose knowledge of China came mainly through mass media soundbites might imagine would be on offer. News broadcasts on the PRC have, since the Tiananmen crackdown, tended to focus on the fact that while the Party has been making dramatic reforms on the economic front, strict political control has remained the order of the day. It is certainly true that the Communist Party can still behave brutally toward groups and individuals it views as threats to its monopoly on power, and that the regime strives to censor discussion of various taboo subjects, from Tibetan independence to the Falun Gong sect. But framing the China story as one of rapid economic change combined with complete political stasis can lead outsiders to underestimate the extent to which cultural and intellectual life has been changing in the PRC. To be fair, the Western mass media has sometimes paid attention to the impact of foreign popular culture, mentioning the popularity of the Harry Potter books, Hollywood movies, and so forth. But there is much more to the cultural story, as Xianfeng's diverse stock attests. It includes translations of foreign works of fiction and non-fiction by all kinds of authors. It also includes Chinese art books of a sort that would not have been seen in Mao's day, when all creative work needed to serve political purposes and defend clearly articulated lines. The first purchase I made at Xianfeng, for example, was a book on Shanghai's many layers by photojournalist Zhang Yao. It is filled with interesting photographic experiments with color and framing, as well as innovative efforts to integrate impressionistic text with striking visuals. It has no explicit political stance on the cities of China today.

There are unusual things about many sections of the two stores, but it has been the "Philosophie" shelves that have struck me as most unlike anything I remembered from the 1980s—and even less like bookstore shelves in Mao's day. In the early 1970s, Mao's works (and those of Marx and Lenin) were virtually the only philosophical tracts offered for sale, and when I first went to China in 1986 the philosophy books available were nearly all Marxist or at least neo-Marxist. Now, however, the best bookstores, such as Xianfeng and its Beijing and Shanghai counterparts, routinely contain translations of works such as Bertrand Russell's *History of Western Philosophy*, books by Hayek and Heidegger, and social theory samplers that let readers know what foreign scholars have been up to (one I saw in 2002 had excerpts by Habermas, Bourdieu, and Giddens). A book by Amartya Sen was on display in a Xianfeng branch in 2002, as was one entitled (optimistically perhaps) *Understanding Foucault*. Literary critics such as Barthes (whose works have sold many more copies in Chinese than in French) are also represented.

What would Mao's verdict on Xianfeng be? Would he think it proof that the Party has gone astray, lapsing into an anything goes approach to knowledge and information and catering to bourgeois decadent tastes, so that the final fall of communism in China is sure to come soon? This is certainly one possibility. There are, however, two others. The first is that spending time in Xianfeng might fill Mao with nostalgia for the days of his youth. That was an era, after all, when Chinese intellectuals were drawn by turns toward various theoretical perspectives coming from outside their own land and when public lectures by the likes of American educator and philosopher John Dewey and Indian Nobel Prize–winning writer Rabindranath Tagore drew large crowds.

Mao's second alternative reaction might be that Xianfeng's existence proved that his successors are, in fact, quite clever, quite good students of his theories. This is because, on close inspection, Mao would realize that there are no books on the shelves that directly criticize Communist rule, suggest that Tibet should be independent, or showcase the thought of famous dissidents. He would also remember that one of his famous adages held that "power comes from the mouth of a gun." Perhaps, he might conclude, today's leaders have simply made a calculated decision that keeping control of the guns (and keeping growth rates high) is all that really matters, and that as long as these things are done there is no harm in giving people more attractive places to buy their books and more choices about what to read. Making this concession to students (a notoriously troublesome group in Mao's lifetime and since) might even keep them from taking to the streets, at least for a while.

3. All the Coffee in China

In their 1994 best-seller, *China Wakes,* Nicholas Kristof and Sheryl WuDunn describe the competing pull of two basic story lines as they reported from Beijing for the *New York Times* in the wake of the Tiananmen crisis of 1989. Sometimes, the most important story seemed the brutal methods that a decaying dynasty was using to retain its monopoly on power. At other moments, though, the country's booming economy stood out as the more significant story to track. Who better symbolized the newest New China, the husband-and-wife team of Pulitzer Prize–winning reporters mused: the prisoner in the *laogai* (Chinese gulag) or the poor farmer turned millionaire? As the century turned and both high growth rates and repressive political policies continued, these two story lines continued to seem compelling to many commentators. Increasingly, though, three additional China tales began to compete for headline space:

The resurgence of nationalism—symbolized by the anti-American demonstrations of 1999, the nastier anti-Japanese street actions of early 2005, and excitement over things such as the upcoming 2008 Beijing Olympics.

The spread of consumerism in step with global trends—symbolized by the arrival of satellite dishes and various new sorts of sites of consumption.

New kinds of protests—symbolized by everything from the 1999 sit-in by members of the Falun Gong sect, to the early 2002 demonstrations by laid-off workers in Northeast China who felt they were being left behind in the drive to privatize the economy, to the late 2005 protests in a South China village, during which paramilitary police fired on residents who were protesting government plans to build a power plant on their land.

Each of these basic story lines, when handled well, sheds light on the PRC today. And yet something has struck me on recent trips to China that has no place in any of them. This is the renewed importance of local pride and local identity in the lives of urban Chinese. Ironically, attachment to particular cities has probably never been stronger than it is in the current era of revived nationalism and rampant globalization.

I first became interested in this general phenomenon—and the special forms it takes in Shanghai, the Chinese city I know best and visit most often—when I returned to the PRC in 1996 after an eight-year absence. I was struck by two contrasts between the billboards and signs I saw on the streets then and those I remembered from the 1980s. The most obvious change was that much more public space was given over to logos and phrases associated with imported products and activities. Everywhere you turned it seemed there were ads for KFC or karaoke, cognac or Coca Cola. But there was a second shift unrelated to commerce. In the 1980s, the streets were still filled, as they had been for decades, with placards and posters extolling the virtues of the Communist Party and its national policies. Some of these were around in 1996, but now they had to vie for attention with displays that sung the praises of specific cities. For every billboard calling on all Chinese to strive to make China a great nation, it seemed, there were two that exhorted the citizens of Beijing or Shanghai or Chongqing to make their metropolis a first-class city.

On subsequent visits, such as the 2002 one I described in the previous chapter that first took me to the Xianfeng Bookstore, I have continued to notice this shift in the use of public space to promote locales and I have also been struck by a complementary development in the world of publishing. The shelves of Shanghai bookstores are now filled with works of local history, including collections of photographs that detail the fashions and lifestyles of the treaty-port era (1843–1943), during which the city was divided into foreign-run and Chinese-run districts. This in itself is not a complete departure from the 1980s, as local history was already a thriving cottage industry in Shanghai and other cities then. But in works published before the 1990s, the stories of particular urban centers tended to be folded neatly into larger national narratives. The central storyline for pre-1949 events hardly varied from village to village and city to city. With every rural locale, the main focus was on how the Chinese people bravely fought, with guidance from the Communist Party, to resist the landlords and the feudalism these powerful men represented. With every city, the main focus was on how workers, with Communist Party guidance, stood up to capitalist exploitation. The one twist added with certain coastal cities, such as Shanghai and Tianjin (the port closest to Beijing), was that patriots and revolutionaries there were portrayed as having fought both capitalist exploitation and a humiliating "treaty port system" that made it possible for foreigners to set up self-governing enclaves on Chinese soil. Now, by contrast, many works approach the local past as intrinsically fascinating or important; they no longer reduce it to just one distinctive piece in a grand patriotic puzzle. And in Shanghai at least the treaty-port era's legacy is currently presented as a complex mixture of the good (cultural and economic cosmopolitanism and engagement with the world) and bad (political subordination to Japan and the West).

On recent trips to China, I have also been struck by how many new books focus on comparing and contrasting individual Chinese cities. Especially popular are those that delineate the allegedly night-and-day differences between Beijing people (stereotyped as stodgy or honest, politically astute or politically obsessed, depending on one's perspective) and Shanghai people (stereotyped as hedonistic or fashionable, money-grubbing or creatively entrepreneurial). These works revisit an early-twentieth-century debate over the relative merits of Jingpai (capital faction) and Haipai (coastal faction) attitudes and styles.

Interestingly, as I learned during a 1999 visit that began just before and ended soon after NATO bombs hit the Chinese Embassy in Belgrade, this renewed competition between locales can even add surprising twists to moments of nationalist fervor. When I arrived in Shanghai on May 10, 1999, after observing rowdy anti-NATO protests in Beijing on May 9, I remarked to an old Shanghainese friend and to new acquaintances (such as a college student I got to know when we noticed that we were taking photographs of the same wall posters) that I felt much less hostility toward Americans in their metropolis than I had in the capital. This was almost invariably interpreted as an invitation to expound upon the overall superiority of Shanghai. Beijing people are too dogmatic and jingoistic, many people told me, whereas Shanghai people, though just as patriotic (there were protests in that city too), are more cosmopolitan and more likely to make "governments are governments but people are people" their motto. Yes, your country's policies have infuriated us, several people told me, from taxi drivers to bookstore attendants, but this doesn't mean Shanghainese like us can't remain friends—and do business—with individual Americans.

My subsequent trips to Shanghai have convinced me that just as local pride can give particular inflections to expressions of nationalism, it can do the same for transnational fads. The coming of Starbucks, which first opened branches in Beijing in 1999 and Shanghai in 2000, illustrates this. Westerners often assume that a Starbucks is a Starbucks is a Starbucks—and the menus and decor of the Chinese branches are very like those of their American counterparts. Yet Starbucks branches occupy very different niches not just in the cultural landscape of the United States as opposed to China but that of Beijing as opposed to Shanghai. For example, controversy broke out in the capital when a branch opened at the edge of the Forbidden City, the former palace that is now a museum. But Shanghai people took it in stride when one opened in Xintiandi (New Heaven and Earth), an upscale dining and shopping quarter, even though that outlet is right around the corner from the hallowed site of the Communist Party's founding congress. In addition, the Beijing and Shanghai stores vie for clients with different sorts of new Chinese-owned establishments. In the capital, some of the main competitors are old or newly opened but old-style teahouses of the sort in which, at least in the popular imagination, Confucian scholars once gathered to talk about poetry and the Classics. In Shanghai, on the other hand, there is a different mix. There are some old-style teahouses, to be sure, but they seem less important competitors to Starbucks than other sorts of establishments: teahouses with walls devoted to displays of experimental art, for instance, Japanese-style coffeehouses, and, above all, cafés designed to evoke memories of the 1920s and 1930s, remembered as a time when the metropolis was a fashionable and heavily Westernized Paris of the East.

When strolling its streets today, tourists and residents alike are invited to enter places with tacky names such as The Real Shanghai Café. And inside these venues, as well as at establishments that try in subtler and more graceful ways to cash in on the local nostalgia craze, the walls are often plastered with black-and-white or sepia-toned photographs of the city in its pre-communist heyday as an international metropolis. One of the nicest of the new cafés to use its interior décor to encourage visitors to think they have traveled back in time is even located inside one of the most important architectural landmarks dating from that period, the one-time headquarters of the Hongkong and Shanghai Bank. In Shanghai, in other words, but *not* Beijing, the arrival of Starbucks in 2000—and the arrival a bit earlier with the branches of fancy Japanese coffeehouse chains that dot the city—seemed simultaneously a novelty and a resumption of an old cosmopolitan trajectory that was interrupted for a time.

Is all this discussion of cafés just a case of a coffee-lover making too much of the fact that there are now scores of places he can get a good cup of cappuccino in a city that served little but instant when he lived there in the mid-1980s? Maybe. But recent visits to the Shanghai History Museum, which is made up of carefully designed displays of well-crafted wax figures and dioramas, suggests otherwise. One of its exhibits portrays a café scene circa 1930. At one table, we see several young Shanghainese men, all dressed in Western

A street in what was formerly the French Concession section of Shanghai.
Photograph by the author.

Postcard showing a display of wax figures at the Shanghai History Museum in the basement of the Pearl of the Orient Tower. *From the author's collection, purchased in 2002 (no copyright information available).*

suits, drinking coffee and carrying on a spirited discussion (of the relative strengths and weaknesses of Jingpai and Haipai novelists?). Nearby is another table where a Chinese man and a man from India are conversing (a nod to the poet-philosopher Rabindranath Tagore's famous visit to Shanghai eighty some years ago?).

The decision to include scenes like this and others without clear political meaning in a museum devoted to the local past is one that would not have been made in the 1980s, since these scenes have no direct links to issues of national import such as the anti-imperialist struggles of the 1910s through 1940s in which Shanghai people of various classes played leading roles. As an astute Western colleague pointed out after a visit to this museum, however, there is something still more remarkable about it than what its tableaus contain. This is something that is missing from the written materials in the museum that recount Shanghai's pre-1949 history: any mention of the Communist Party. This lack may tell us as much as any presence about the resurgence of localism in born-again global Shanghai. One of the main driving forces behind the resurgence of local identity, after all, is a desire to find new bases of loyalty and affection to fill the void left by the cynicism that many Chinese now feel toward a system that seems irredeemably corrupt and a regime whose ideology seems less coherent and less compelling with each passing year.

4. The Generalissimo Would Not Be Amused

Many American China specialists of my generation and nearly all of those who are older than me spent at least a little bit of time in Taipei, Taiwan's leading metropolis, before ever setting foot in the PRC. A large number of them did a significant part of their Chinese language study in that Taiwanese metropolis. In addition, most of them returned to Taipei at later points to attend conferences or use archival materials that Generalissimo Chiang Kai-shek and other Nationalist Party leaders took with them when they retreated to Taiwan from the mainland in the late 1940s. This meant that when many of my Chinese studies colleagues finally did get an opportunity to visit or live in cities such as Beijing, they quite naturally found themselves using Taipei as a point of reference. Especially if their first PRC trip took place before the mid- to late-1980s, the result was that they often thought of mainland cities as comparatively backward, at least in terms of access to consumer goods and efficient libraries, though some were positively impressed by the fact that less of a gulf separated the lifestyles of rich and poor in PRC than in

Taiwanese urban centers. Even Shanghai, which before 1949 was sometimes described as the most "modern" city in East Asia but by the 1980s lacked the sort of transportation and communication infrastructure found in Taipei, seemed stuck at an early point on a modernization timeline along which Taiwan's main cities had moved quite far. And the contrasts related not just to material goods and infrastructure: a political scientist friend—the same one who made the remark about the Shanghai history museum noted in the previous chapter—told me, for instance, that the loosening up of the PRC public sphere that occurred in the late 1980s and resumed in the mid-1990s reminded her of shifts in Taiwan's public sphere in the late 1970s.

My own experience has been quite different from that of the colleagues alluded to above, because I did not do language work in Taiwan, went to the mainland to do my dissertation research in the mid-1980s, and didn't make it to Taipei until I was invited to attend conferences and give lectures there in 2004 and 2005. As a result, I had spent a lot of time in Shanghai and also stayed for shorter periods in various other mainland cities long before I first set foot in Taiwan. Hence it was with eyes trained to see Chinese urban life through a lens shaped by spending time in mainland cities, and particularly my various stays in Shanghai, that I first looked at Taipei—not the other way around. Throughout both of the trips I have made to Taipei, I have continually contrasted things I have seen there with comparable things I have seen in Shanghai and other PRC urban centers—and I have been aware that, in doing so, I have been reversing the type of gaze through which many of my colleagues first viewed mainland cities.

Another kind of reversal has accompanied this different mode of comparing cities on opposite sides of the Taiwan Straits: rather than thinking in terms of mainland cities "catching up" to Taipei, I have sometimes seen sights that suggested it was the ROC capital that had not moved as far along a modernizing timeline. It is true that, when I finally made it to Taiwan, the bamboo-shaped edifice known as Taipei 101, one of the only true skyscrapers in the ROC's capital city, held the distinction of being the tallest building on earth. Still, I hardly thought of Taipei as further along any kind of timeline than Shanghai, since by 2004 Pudong had several buildings almost as tall (and one in the works that will be even taller) and a magnetic levitation (maglev) train, which rockets riders at speeds that far surpass even those of Japan's famed Shinkansen, or bullet trains.

One of the places I went sight-seeing in Taiwan that made me particularly aware of the peculiarity of my mainland-shaped gaze was the Chiang Kai-shek Memorial. In a curious bit of timing, the deaths of the Generalissimo and of his mainland archrival, Chairman Mao, took place less than 18 months apart, with the former dying in April of 1975, the latter in September of 1976. This meant that discussions of how to commemorate the two paramount leaders took place nearly simultaneously in Taipei and Beijing, as did the building of monuments in these capital cities. And the parallels between the deaths of the two leaders went beyond this fluke of timing, as Frederic Wakeman showed in a 1985 essay, "Revolutionary Rites: The Remains of Chiang Kai-shek and Mao Tse-tung." According to Wakeman, there were many similarities in the mid-1970s between the efforts made in Taipei to honor the Generalissimo and in Beijing to honor the Chairman. Some of the same phrases were used in speeches honoring the fallen leaders, for example, and the monuments built to commemorate their lives took analogous forms. Thanks to memories of that essay (which made a particularly strong impact since its author was then my dissertation advisor), and even more to memories of the visit to the Mao Mausoleum I made in 1987, my viewing of the Chiang Kai-shek Memorial inspired a string of thoughts about similarities and differences between the shrines honoring the Generalissimo and the Chairman.

One thing that struck me as a dramatic contrast was the giant statue of Chiang Kai-shek that stood at the top of a staircase of 89 steps (one for each year in the Generalissimo's long life) at the Taipei memorial. I knew that, unlike Mao, Chiang's body was not on display in a glass case.* Still, I half-expected to see him lying permanently

---

* It is kept a few miles outside of the city in a granite tomb, awaiting the day when the Communists fall and Chiang can be returned to the mainland to be buried in Nanjing near his brother-in-law and mentor, Sun Yat-sen. The body of his son, Chiang Ching-Kuo, who followed him as President of the ROC, is also in Taiwan awaiting transportation to the mainland for final burial. The Generalissimo's wife, Soong Mei-ling, who died in New York, is due for the same treatment, but her corpse awaits it in the United States.

The Chiang Kai-shek Memorial, Taipei. *Photograph by the author.*

in state when I got to the memorial. It was disconcerting to see instead a massive representation of the in-life generally stern-looking Generalissimo smiling down on visitors as beatifically as any Buddha or bodhisattva. And there were some other intriguing contrasts between the way the Generalissimo, as opposed to Mao, is commemorated. For example, a claim is made at the Chiang Kai-shek Memorial that the man it honors was a descendant of the Duke of Zhou, an aristocratic figure whom Confucius lauded as a model of virtue during an early Chinese golden age. At the Mao Mausoleum, by contrast, there is definitely no effort to place the Chairman within a lineage that includes ancient members of a feudal noble class!

One of the things that stood out as similar to as opposed to different from what I had seen in Beijing when I went to visit Mao were the exhibits inside the Taipei memorial that provided a visual and textual rendition of the Nationalist Party version of the story of the Chinese Revolution. The heroes and villains are not the same in the versions of revolutionary history on display in Taipei and Beijing—in fact, with the crucial exception of Sun Yat-sen, who is honored on both sides of the Taiwan Straits, twentieth-century historical figures celebrated in the PRC are likely to be vilified in the ROC and vice versa. And yet, leaving aside this important dissimilarity, the basic thrust of the narratives of self-sacrifice and national redemption are much the same.

It is true, of course, that some elements of the exhibits at the Chiang Kai-shek Memorial could easily remind a viewer of patriotic displays in non-Chinese settings. This was brought to my attention by Michael McGerr, an Indiana University colleague specializing in American history, who was in Taipei to attend the same conference that had brought me there, and with whom I toured the shrine to the Generalissimo. Perhaps because he already had the era of the American Civil War on his mind, and due to the ways that the giant Chiang Kai-shek statue we saw resembled not just Buddha but also the Honest Abe of the Lincoln Memorial in Washington, D.C., his first comment on the paintings of the Generalissimo we saw inside was that they looked a lot like canvases showing General Grant leading his troops into battle. Once he pointed this out, it was indeed

striking to me how much the visual grammar of these representations of the Chinese Civil War of 1945 1949 resembled ones of the
much earlier American Civil War. And yet, they still reminded me
more of exhibits in the Beijing Museum of Revolutionary History,
located right near the Mao Mausoleum in Tiananmen Square.

Just as memories of what I had seen in mainland cities shaped my
response to the Chiang Kai-shek Memorial and many other sights I
saw in Taipei (from the entry gates to local universities that were almost identical to their counterparts in Beijing to the inside of the
wonderful Eslite Bookstore, which struck me as a much grander version of Nanjing's Xianfeng), previous experiences in places such as
Shanghai also affected my other senses during my first trips to Taiwan. Olfactory sensations, for example, sometimes triggered mainland memories. Here, I'll just refer to the one that was most pleasant. When I went to a highly—and justly—touted restaurant called
Dingtaifeng (sometimes romanized as "Dintaifeng") in the heart of
Taipei, as I inhaled the aroma of steaming *xiaolongbao* (literally:
little steamer dumplings), a Shanghainese specialty (sometimes
called "soup dumplings" in the U.S., since they have liquid inside
the wrapping), I felt that I had been transported across the Taiwan
Straits to Shanghai. Closing my eyes, I felt as if were in one of two
favorite spots in that city by the Huangpu. The eighth-floor dining
room of the Peace Hotel, an art deco riverfront structure dating
from the treaty-port era (when it was called the Cathay Hotel). Or
the Lao Fandian (literally: Old Restaurant), which is located in the
oldest part of Shanghai, a district that was already a bustling center of
urban life in the sixteenth century. Why? Because those were two of
the places I had first eaten *xiaolongbao* in the 1980s, and are places
I've regularly returned to whenever I've been back in Shanghai.

Sounds also triggered reflections on ways that Taipei was like or
unlike mainland urban centers. For example, each time I took a taxi
in Taipei, I found myself listening to the things the driver said and
to the sounds that came from the tape deck or radio he had on,
thinking and comparing what I heard to what I had heard during
my rides in mainland cabs. When I caught a cab at the Chiang Kai-
shek Memorial Airport upon arriving in Taipei in September of
2005, for example, I was reminded of things that the driver of the

first taxi I ever took in the mainland had done to make his Western passengers feel at home. Namely, he had put on a tape of Italian opera music (Pavarotti perhaps, as he was very popular in China at the time), not knowing (how could he?) that our tastes ran to folk, rock, and country songs much more than to arias. Similarly—but with a twist—the Taipei driver started fiddling around with his radio as soon as I got in his cab in 2005, trying to find a station with something on that I would understand and, ideally, like.

Unfortunately, the first thing he came to in the language he correctly assumed was my native tongue was a fairly rudimentary but somewhat specialized English lesson, and I spent several minutes quietly trying to be polite while two bland voices taught their listeners the vocabulary words they would find most helpful when taking a tour of an American college campus. (Sample questions listeners were encouraged to repeat included the following: "Where is the dining hall?" "Which building is the library?" "Does this school have fraternities and sororities?") Unable to take any more of this, I told him in Chinese—the same language I had used, by the way, when telling him upon entering his cab that I wished to be taken to the Academia Sinica—that I would prefer to listen to some music, if that was okay with him. He said that was fine and began switching stations, settling after a bit (due to his preferences or what he imagined were mine?) on one that had an expat deejay from the United States who seemed to be stuck in a time-warp, as the words he used came straight out of the 1970s (or perhaps were meant as a parody pastiche of late psychedelic, heavy metal, and early disco slang), yet the music was a mixture of Cantonese pop and American hip-hop.

I was so exhausted from the flight that when the Taipei taxi driver settled on this pop station, I decided to just sit back and listen—though I later regretted that I had not asked him some questions that it brought to mind. For example, I became curious later as to whether the driver thought that ordinary Americans (even ordinary American deejays) routinely talked excitedly about what a great idea it was for a radio station to hold a "bikini party" in a ritzy downtown hotel, to which no woman would be allowed entrance unless she was wearing a skimpy two-piece swimsuit. On my visits to the mainland, after all, I had often asked cab drivers what their image was of the

United States, and had sometimes pointed out that I thought exposure to Sylvester Stallone movies (the "Rambo" series is well known in the PRC) and violent television cop shows had given them what seemed to me a misleading impression of ordinary American life.

Though I missed an opportunity with that cab driver to find out information that would help me get a feel for one way that Taipei and mainland cities might differ—namely, if members of one occupational group in the former had less exaggerated views of the U.S. than their counterparts in the latter—there were other instances in which I made better use of rides in ROC taxis. For example, on a couple of occasions I made a point of trying to test claims I had heard about increased Taiwanese tourism to the mainland and the rise of Taiwanese investment in the PRC, which has led to such things as the opening of a branch of Dingtaifeng in Shanghai, a city now estimated to have hundreds of thousands of ROC citizens living and working within its borders. I would ask drivers whether they had ever been to the mainland, for example, and whether they knew anyone who did business with or worked for a PRC firm. The most striking answer I got: "Have I ever been to the mainland? No. But my wife works in Shanghai."

One thing that struck me when I pondered that cab driver's comments later was that his wife—I never found out her profession, as the matter-of-factness of the tone in which he told me where she worked left me speechless right up until the time a few minutes later when we got to my destination—would have initially viewed Shanghai through a lens much like that some of my American colleagues in Chinese studies had. She had probably compared and contrasted the look and feel of urban life there to experiences living in Taipei.* So, not only did my tendency to view Taipei through a lens provided by mainland visits (as opposed to the reverse) set me apart from dozens of American academics, but it also set me apart from an exponentially larger number of residents of Taiwan.

---

* Though, of course, unlike my colleagues, she would have first encountered a Shanghai inhabited by a great many other people from Taiwan, whereas in the 1980s at least there were at most hundreds—not hundreds of thousands—of Americans residing in or passing through the city at any given time.

And yet, by the time I finished my second visit to Taipei, I had become convinced that my way of looking at and thinking about that city was not quite so unusual after all. Why? Because I heard various people mention the recent rise in the number of mainland tourists (and mainland wives of Taiwanese men) coming to Taiwan. This led me to remember and make new sense of scattered comments I had overheard in Chinese when looking at the exhibits in the Chiang Kai-shek Memorial. No Chinese-speaking visitors to the exhibit had come right out and said that a given painting reminded him or her of a painting on display in the Museum of Revolutionary History. But one had told the other members of his tour group to note that, even though Mao had also been fighting the Japanese in the 1930s, the caption on a certain photograph made no mention of that.

But what really brought home to me just how common PRC visitors—who see Taipei sights through eyes shaped by mainland experience—are becoming was a menu that I saw outside of a café near the Chiang Kai-shek Memorial. There was nothing special about the items of food and drink it contained, no special culinary accommodation of travelers from the mainland. There was, though, something very unusual about the way the prices were listed. For every item you could order, the cost in National Taiwan Dollars was given, but in another column so too was its cost in Renminbi, the currency of the PRC. When I pointed out this curious thing to my waiter and asked why both currencies were listed, he replied somewhat enigmatically that it was because of where the café was located—and then, to indicate what he meant about the location, pointed over toward the Chiang Kai-shek Memorial. He seemed to think that I was a bit slow not to realize that one sight PRC tourists would want to see was that shrine to the Generalissimo.

Both before I left Taipei and since returning to the U.S., I've asked several China specialists what they think the menu with the two prices means. I've also asked whether they think anyone actually pays with PRC bills that have Mao's face on them—alas, I did not think to ask my waiter that simple follow-up question. My colleagues have given me a range of answers. Some think Renminbi might actually be used occasionally. Others have suggested that listing the prices in two currencies could be done as an aid to travelers from the mainland, giving them practical help figuring out, without doing the conversions in their head, how cheap or expensive an item is. A third explanation is that listing the cost in Renminbi is a gesture to show that PRC tourists are welcome in the establishment—like a British restaurant in Dover flying a French flag.

For my part, I lean toward the second and even more so the third of these explanations. I just have trouble imagining the café regularly getting and finding some way to exchange currency from a country with which Taiwan is, in formal political terms, still at such odds—though I can see how, for example, that cab driver's wife I heard about might have found it very convenient to get hold of some Renminbi before her first trip to Shanghai. Moreover, using prices to convey openness to tourists from a particular land seems quite clever—especially in light of the fact that one's choices are limited in this particular setting, since in the heart of Taipei a PRC flag definitely still cannot be flown in public without repercussions of some sort. Whatever the reason it lists its prices in two currencies, that café near the Chiang Kai-shek Memorial raises interesting questions to ponder. For example, if the Generalissimo's corpse could magically be made to hear, what would Chiang Kai-shek think if he was told that, in theory at least, one can now use money printed either in Taiwan or the mainland to buy a latte or piece of cake in a Taipei establishment? Would he think this an encouraging sign that the reunification of the country he had long dreamt of was somehow about to take place? Or would the thought of bills bearing the visage of his archrival Mao showing up in Taipei set his corpse spinning in the above-ground granite box that it lies in while waiting for its long-delayed triumphant return to the mainland?

PART TWO

THE INSCRUTABLE WEST

The view from atop Notre Dame. *Photograph by Gina Bock, used by permission.*

5. Searching the Stars for Emily Hahn

St. Louis, Missouri, has a lot going for it: a dramatic location on the banks of a famous river, an impressive icon (the giant metal waterfront Arch erected in the 1960s to commemorate the role the city once played as gateway to the American West), and a rich cultural history that reached an early peak when it hosted the World's Fair and Olympics in 1904. In addition, a surprising number of notable contributors to both highbrow and popular cultural genres were born in St. Louis; a full list of its native sons and daughters includes everyone from poet T. S. Eliot, to comedian Dick Gregory, to novelist Kate Chopin, to film star Betty Grable, to rocker Chuck Berry, to jazz chanteuse Josephine Baker, to the prolific writer Emily Hahn, author of more than one hundred *New Yorker* essays and scores of books, including a biography of Chiang Kai-shek and *The Soong Sisters,* a more famous work that tells the life stories of the Generalissimo's charismatic wife, Soong Mei-ling, and her two sisters (one of whom married Sun Yat-sen, the other of whom married China's richest banker). And yet, despite these claims to fame and despite having once been the grandest city in the Midwest and the fourth largest metropolis in the United States, St. Louis has long had an odd inferiority complex, especially vis-à-vis Chicago, the upstart city to the north that also first attracted global attention by holding an international exhibition, the Columbian Exposition of 1893. Many locals now imagine that people in other places, when they think of St. Louis at all, view it as a city well past its prime that has only one real claim to fame: the fact that it once served as a starting point for journeys toward the Pacific such as that the Lewis and Clark Expedition set out upon two hundred years ago.

For some residents, this image problem is a cause of anxiety. Others, however, treat it with more detachment, and self-deprecating comments have become a local specialty. There is, for example, the ironic boast sometimes heard in St. Louis these days that, thanks to its fortunate position in the middle of the country, the city has gotten all the best that America has to offer: the efficiency of the South and the warmth and gentility of the North.

This vision of St. Louis—as a great but underappreciated city that charmingly does not take itself too seriously—is one that formed in my mind, in any case, as I read up on the metropolis in the fall of 2003 while preparing to travel there to take part in a conference. I had been to St. Louis before that, on short trips, in part simply because it was one of the biggest and most interesting urban centers within easy driving distance of Bloomington, Indiana, home to the university that employed me from August of 1991 through June of 2006. But I had not made much effort to learn about the city's past before those earlier visits. While getting ready for the 2003 trip, though, I felt differently for three reasons. First, I was working on a book about Shanghai, and that city's high profile and ultimately successful campaign to host the 2010 World Expo had made me interested in how cities that had previously staged comparable global events were affected by the experience. Second, I had grown fascinated by the writings and life story of one of the famous St. Louis natives mentioned above, Emily Hahn, who was born there just a year after its World's Fair yet almost lived to see the dawn of the twenty-first century. My interest in this long-lived author, like my interest in cities that had hosted international exhibitions, had a

Shanghai connection. She had lived there in the 1930s, and Shanghai served as the setting for "The Big Smoke," one of her many *New Yorker* essays. (Whether this essay is one of her best as well as one of her best known, I am not sure, as I have still only read a fraction of her total output, but it certainly has one of her most memorable opening lines: "Though I had always wanted to be an opium addict, I can't claim that as the reason I went to China.")

A final reason I decided to find out a bit about the city in advance of my 2003 visit—by dipping into standard tourist publications and more specialized books such as Cuoco and Gass's *Literary St. Louis: A Guide* and Lee Ann Sandweiss's *Seeking St. Louis: Voices from a River City, 1670–2000*—was the nature of the conference I was going to attend. This was the biennial gathering of an organization that has a rather cumbersome and somewhat misleading name: the Society for American City and Regional Planning History (SACRPH). Though one might not think this from the name, this is actually a very eclectic urban studies association, some of whose members are not particularly interested in planning per se and do historical or culturally minded work on cities located in Europe or Asia as opposed to the Americas. What, then, is the common thread connecting their interests? According to a comment made during the 2003 St. Louis meetings by Eric Sandweiss—a colleague of mine at Indiana University, who was at the time the incoming president of SACRPH and the one who convinced me to serve as a discussant for a panel at the conference—it is a shared interest in the ways that a sense of place shapes urban history and the experience of city life. To go to a gathering of such people (even as an interested outsider who did not belong to the association) without spending some time thinking in advance about the particular urban setting in which it was to be held just would not have seemed right.

Now, as it turned out, the papers presented at the panel for which I was discussant all focused on places located far from the Mississippi (London, Boston, New York, and Jakarta, to be precise), but I was nonetheless glad during the meetings that before coming I had done my St. Louis homework. Reading around in works such as the two stimulating literary collections mentioned above—both published in 2000 by the Missouri Historical Society—helped me put into perspective some of the presentations and hallway conversations I heard, more than a few of which dwelt on the special characteristics of St. Louis and its image problem.

That preparation also gave me a context for making sense of the event that was, for me, the highlight of the whole conference: a learned, politically engaged, and often also laugh-out-loud funny lunchtime talk comparing and contrasting the official and hidden histories of St. Louis delivered by George Lipsitz. In his address, this cultural historian, who lived in St. Louis for a time but went on to teach Ethnic Studies at the University of California at San Diego and then American Studies at the University of California at Santa Cruz, moved smoothly between topics ranging from labor strikes to the blues, Mark Twain's ideas about the Mississippi River to the destruction of old landmarks and the creation of civic monuments. The politics of race was a recurring theme. He noted, for example, the ironic fact that just when the city was mocked in some circles (and, typically, poked fun at itself) for having the worst baseball team in the still whites-only American League, its Negro League club included some of the most talented ballplayers of the day. And he told us of Josephine Baker, invited back to perform in her hometown after gaining fame in Paris, refusing to stay in the very hotel in which our meetings were being held unless other blacks were allowed into that then-still-segregated establishment. Another theme of Lipsitz's talk was the distinctive character traits that seemed to him to show up in disproportionate numbers of St. Louis residents, such as an admirable sort of contrariness manifested in a fondness for irreverent gestures.

In addition to helping me during the conference, reading up on St. Louis gave me a special appreciation for one of the curious local sights that I made a point to seek out—just to see if it contained any reference to Emily Hahn. This is the "St. Louis Walk of Fame," which is made up of a series of stars placed on the ground, à la those in Hollywood, to celebrate famous people who were either born in the city, moved there when young, or lived in St. Louis during particularly important moments in their careers. Thus there are stars for three Pulitzer Prize–winning authors with varied ties to the city: Maya Angelou (who was born there), Tennessee Williams (who moved to St. Louis in time to go to local high schools), and William Inge (who grew up elsewhere in the Midwest but began his career as a dramatist while teaching at Washington University). A walk of this sort—which also includes stars honoring jazz great Miles Davis, who moved to nearby Alton, Illinois, in infancy, and Charles Lindbergh, who once worked flying a mail route between this metropolis and Chicago and made his famous Atlantic crossing in a plane called *The Spirit of St. Louis*—may not seem at first the kind of thing a place with an inferiority complex would do. Upon reflection, though, the 1991 creation of the Walk of Fame might have been triggered in part by just the sort of feeling that St. Louis does not get the respect it deserves that I came across in my readings. Would a city full of confidence about its cultural legacy, I asked myself, have bothered to create something like this?

I am still mulling this rhetorical question, but I have settled a more basic empirical one: at least as of 2003 there was no star for Emily Hahn on the most often examined stretch of St. Louis sidewalk (and a late-2006 foray into cyberspace to check relevant websites indicated one was not added in the following three years). In some ways, this is not surprising. At one time, she was quite famous. This was largely due to her *New Yorker* articles and books, which ran the gamut of fiction and non-fiction, including everything from the biographical works mentioned above, to a string of popular travel accounts-cum-memoirs (*Africa to Me, China to Me,* and *England to Me* among them). It was also, though, linked to her personal life, which was sometimes considered quite scandalous, as during World War II when she became pregnant by Charles Boxer, who would eventually become her husband and a leading historian of maritime Asia, but was at the time a British military officer based in Hong Kong and married to someone else. Still, by 1991, hers was not a household name like that of Chuck Berry (who has a star, of course), nor had any of her writings acquired the canonical status of Chopin's *The Awakening* or Eliot's *The Wasteland,* which ensured them their spots of honor on their hometown's Walk of Fame.

While it is certainly understandable that Hahn would be passed over, I nonetheless became convinced by reading her *Times and Places* (a collection of autobiographical pieces from the *New Yorker* that I brought with me on that 2003 trip), that her absence from the Walk of Fame is unfortunate. This is not just because she was a talented writer but also because her actions and personality, as they come through in *Times and Places,* reflect what I have come to think of as quintessential St. Louis themes. For starters, Hahn certainly had the sort of contrary streak Lipsitz described in his talk. She claimed, for example, that one reason she ended up becoming the first woman to graduate from the University of Wisconsin with a degree in mining engineering was simply to prove wrong the men on campus who had told her that someone of her sex could not possibly handle the rigors of that major. In addition, as befits a St. Louis native, though her later travels took her across oceans, her first big trip was over land from the Mississippi to the Pacific.

Last but not least, she was skilled at poking fun at herself. This shows through in many of her accounts of journeying through Asia and Africa, but my favorite example of her self-deprecating humor is in a chapter of *Times and Places,* "Pilgrim's Progress," which focuses mainly on what happened to her when she finally got back to the U.S. toward the end of World War II. It begins with a brief account of her adventures in Hong Kong in the early 1940s, where she pretended to be Eurasian so that the Japanese occupiers would neither imprison nor deport her. (Boxer was a prisoner of war held in miserable conditions. While there, she could slip him food from time to time.) Eventually, though, she had to leave, and it is after describing her departure from Asia that Hahn's self-mocking begins. She must have become insufferable, she muses, once she got to New York, full of bad habits acquired during her travels and determined to regale her relatives with endless stories about her exploits. Perhaps, though, she notes, this is a common fate for travelers. We do not know what Marco Polo's relatives thought of him, Hahn writes, but she is willing to "bet anything that they found their celebrated kinsman an awful nuisance to have around," due in part to the way "he expected the young people to listen whenever he felt like telling an anecdote."

Continuing in a similar vein, she points to the likelihood that, though we never hear about things that happened after Ulysses got back to Ithaca, it was probably not an unblemished source of joy for Penelope. Of course, Penelope would have been "glad to have him back to rescue her from that difficult situation, but, once the excitement of the homecoming was over, she may well have found it difficult to adjust to him—a man who had grown all too used to the rough life of the seafarer. By day, he would complain that Ithaca was dull and would mope around the estate. By night, he would sleep badly, often starting up out of a nightmare to shout hoarsely about alarms and excursions. Anxious times for Penelope."

Surely, anyone who can write like that deserves a star on the Walk of Fame of any metropolis lucky enough to be able to claim her. With luck, it will only be a matter of time before local residents and tourists who examine this stretch of St. Louis sidewalk can be reminded that Mark Twain was not the only writer of wonderful tales of world travel born by the banks of the Mississippi.

6. Traveling with Twain

I have written essays and given talks about the Boxer Uprising from time to time since the mid-1980s, and I occasionally lecture on U.S.-Chinese relations and the ways that people in these two countries have thought about and treated one another. As a result, the works by Mark Twain that I have turned to most often since starting graduate school more than twenty years ago have been his critical essays on American imperialism (including some that castigate missionaries for their actions in China) and his writings on the treatment of Chinese immigrants to the United States. These works were not, however, what made me a fan of Samuel Clemens. That happened much earlier—in fact, before I had read *anything* he had written. Indeed, I have been a Mark Twain fan since I was six years old, even though I did not encounter a word he wrote before turning ten.

What made me a fan? Well, it was not hearing one of his stories read aloud, as one might expect. Nor was it seeing a play, television show, or film featuring characters such as Huck Finn and Tom

Sawyer that did it. No, what made me a fan was my first trip to Disneyland, where Tom Sawyer's Island immediately became one of my favorite sections of the theme park . I quickly concluded that anyone who could provide the inspiration for such a wondrous place, filled with secret tunnels through the rocks and creaking wooden bridges, was worth admiring. When I finally got around to reading *The Adventures of Tom Sawyer,* I was gratified to discover that Twain really was the special writer that I had imagined him to be. I was also relieved that the characters I met on the page behaved like the ones I had conjured up during Disneyland daydreams.

Things have not always worked out quite this way with expectations formed at Anaheim's famous theme park. Sometimes, the real thing has come far short of living up to the promise of the simulation. Other times, encountering the original has left me feeling that Disney did not do it justice. The mundane business of learning to drive a car, after being thrilled by childhood opportunities to get behind the wheel and go around the Autopia ride's track, fits into the first category, while seeing the Swiss Alps, after being introduced to the faux Matterhorn in Southern California, fits into the second. Most books first encountered in childhood and revisited years later fit someplace in between. While *The Adventures of Tom Sawyer* pleasantly confirmed a set of preconceived notions, encountering other books of Twain's has often worked out quite differently.

When I took a course devoted to the author while a college sophomore, I found that some of the texts we read fit in neatly with images I brought with me into the class. Others, however, most definitely did not. By that point, there was a lot that I knew—or, rather, thought I knew—about the author's life and work. Many different kinds of things had shaped my notions about him—not just those early trips to Disneyland, but also assorted films and television shows, and even some firsthand encounters with Twain's books. Taking the class, I found that some of my notions were simply wrong. For example, I came in thinking of Twain as someone who only wrote short stories and novels. It was a surprise to find out how large a role travel writings and essays had played in establishing his reputation as a writer. And in my mind Twain was linked only with the South and the Midwest, so it was surprising to discover that he had spent important parts of his life in California and on the East Coast, and that he had ventured abroad several times, even going all the way around the world on a lecture tour in the 1890s.

I guess, most of all, I was surprised to find out how many works by Twain had not been transformed into shows or films. The works I read for that class that I had been exposed to in some way beforehand, such as *A Connecticut Yankee in King Arthur's Court* and *The Prince and the Pauper,* were certainly enjoyable. But the books that made the deepest impression on me then were several that I had never heard of before. There was no need to ponder, as I read these, whether *The Wonderful World of Disney* had handled the material well.

One work of this sort that I greatly enjoyed was *Innocents Abroad or The New Pilgrims' Progress,* which was published in 1869 and offers a humorous account of an 1867 trip to Europe and the Middle East that Twain took as part of an early group tour. There was something refreshing about reading works such as *Innocents Abroad.* I was not burdened by considering, as I read, whether a film or television director had captured their essences. Nor did I find myself thinking about the odd choice a studio had made when casting the lead for a cinematic rendition, as happened when I read *Connecticut Yankee* with images of Bing Crosby in my head.

Instead, reading *Innocents Abroad,* which was adapted from letters to newspapers that Twain wrote while taking his tour, I could focus on appreciating the writing simply for its own sake. Well, not quite. The professor teaching the class, though he did a great job of bringing Twain and his times alive, was a bit too obsessed with Freudian ideas for my taste. This meant that his students were told to remain vigilantly on the lookout for the appearance of certain kinds of symbols and images. And we were encouraged to be mindful always of how Twain's humor was linked to a dark view of life and a pessimistic vision of human nature. The professor's injunctions, though, did little to hinder my uncomplicated enjoyment of books like *Innocents Abroad* and others that were previously unknown to me such as *Roughing It,* an often very funny 1872 account of the author's adventures in the American West during the years immediately preceding his trip to Europe and the Middle East. In fact, when I started to reread *Innocents Abroad* several years ago, fittingly enough during a family trip to France (one of the countries described in its pages), I could not remember a single passage that had revealed a Freudian outlook. When I returned to the book some twenty-two years after first encountering it, the only specific passages from it I remembered were silly ones that had made me laugh.

If one section of *Innocents* stuck most in my memory, it was chapter 27 (a chapter that in some editions is aptly titled "Rare Sport—Guying the Guides"), which finds Twain describing, to delirious effect, how he and some mischievous co-conspirators flummoxed one of their innumerable guides. Sick of having various guides in Italy tell them endless stories about Christopher Columbus, assuming that the great "Christo Columbo" was the one Italian about whom all Americans wanted to know everything, Twain and his partners in mischief took to pretending that they had never heard of the explorer. When the guide showed them a document written by Columbus, they merely commented on the poor quality of the penmanship. ("Why, I have seen boys in America only fourteen years old who could write better than that," one of Twain's companions says.) They then asked naively whether this Columbo fellow was dead, a query that greatly irritated the poor guide. So, too, did their irrelevant follow-up questions, such as whether Columbus had died from measles.

It may seem odd to have begun a chapter that is intended to be concerned with the experience of rereading *Innocents Abroad* with references above to such quintessentially twentieth-century phenomena as Disneyland, television shows, and films. After all, Twain's book, in which he often subjects the American travelers in whose company he journeyed to the same sort of humorous scrutiny that he turns on the sites and people of foreign lands, is very much a product of the period in which it was written. That was an era that predated by close to a century the founding of Anaheim's famous theme park and television's rise to prominence. The origins of the cinema lie in the late 1800s, closer to the period of Twain's first crossing of the Atlantic. Even where film is concerned, however, we are dealing with a medium that did not become a powerful shaper of popular images until *Innocents Abroad* had been around for about half a century.

And yet, back in 1869 Twain was already fascinated by the varied responses one could have to first encounters with things to which one had previously been exposed indirectly. Sometimes, he describes his initial encounter with the real thing as a source of disappointment of the sort I felt when I discovered how much more worrisome real driving was than the Autopia version. Consider, for example, "The Turkish Bath Fraud." According to Twain, his first Turkish bath was a terrible, indeed traumatic experience, so shockingly devoid was it of the elegance that literary accounts had led him to anticipate.

In other cases, though, Twain shows us how previous exposure via representations can give a new experience a pleasing sense of familiarity mixed with novelty, akin to what I felt when reading *Tom Sawyer* after being primed for it by Disneyland. He describes "speeding through the streets of Paris" for the first time, all the while "delightfully recognizing certain names and places with which books had long ago made us familiar." Seeing pictures of the Louvre prepared him for the look of the "genuine vast palace" itself; it was "like meeting an old friend when we read *'Rue de Rivoli'* on the street corner"; and he instantly recognized the "brown old Gothic heap" that was Notre Dame, since it was so much "like the pictures" of it he had seen.

In still other cases, he claims, encountering a site about which he thought he knew what to expect in advance could turn out to be nothing short of a revelation. Take, for example, his section on "The Majestic Sphinx," in which he describes seeing for the first time in person an Egyptian icon that was doubtless as familiar to him as the Matterhorn was to me during my Southern California childhood. "After years of waiting, it was before me at last," he writes, and then begins describing its wondrous qualities in a way that makes it clear that he was unprepared for just how impressive he would find it. So taken with it was he that his description of the Sphinx stands out as an unusual part of the book, since in extolling its glories, Twain drops his usual satirical tone and just enthuses.

Sometimes, Twain suggests, only true novelty—a first encounter, devoid of expectations—will do. "One charm of travel" dies for him in Rome, where he finds there is nothing "to feel, to learn, to hear" that others have not already felt, learned, and heard. While Twain makes it clear that he does not yearn for actual discovery—being the first to go somewhere—he hungers occasionally for the next best thing: to see sites that have not inspired artistic creations or made it into guidebooks.

Twain's interest in exploring and teasing humor out of the interplay between expectations and encounters resonates powerfully with contemporary concerns, as does his feeling that having clearly formed images of places in advance can sometimes add to—but sometimes detract from—the experience of travel. Much has been made of late of how important simulations have become in our twenty-first-century lives, and how new media have begun to drown us in representations. And much has also been made of the way that, in the current age, the tourist industry has to play to our desire for both familiarity and the exotic. We want to see firsthand places that we feel we know already, thanks to their appearance in movies, specials on the travel channel, *National Geographic* feature stories, and so on. And yet, as the popularity of "rough guides" show, we also hunger to get off the beaten track at least a bit and come as close to "discovering" things as we can in an era of information overload.

There are many novelties about the current situation, of course, in terms of the specific media that shape in advance our images of distant places and the way we prepare for trips to far-off locales. Before leaving the United States, Americans can now journey into cyberspace not only to find places to stay but also to see images of their future accommodations. We did just this before the four of us set off to France in 2003. Prior to arriving in Paris, my wife showed our two children and me a website that contained a photo of the Parisian apartment she had rented for us. Moreover, sometimes when Americans go abroad, they take with them images of a foreign country formed by more than just what they have read in books and seen on television screens, movie screens, and computer screens. Before our eleven-year-old daughter and fourteen-year-old son ever crossed the Atlantic, for example, they had visited the faux version of France that can be found at Epcot Center. (Just go past Norway and China and if you reach Canada, then you have gone too far.) It remains an open question, though, whether these sorts of novelties mean that a chasm separates travelers of 1867 and 2004 when it comes to the interplay between images and experience. And reading up on the role of simulations in Twain's day has convinced me that the divide between then and now is a much subtler one than it appears at first to be.

Vanessa Schwartz, in her fascinating book, *Spectacular Realities: Early Mass Culture in Fin-de-Siècle Paris,* explains that the nineteenth century, like the twentieth, witnessed the rise of many forms of mass media, from serialized novels to panoramas. And as a result, the mid- to late-1800s were, like the present, a time when the lines between simulations and "reality" were continually being drawn, erased, and blurred in alternately confusing, disturbing, and exhilarating ways.

There is much in Twain's account that illuminates the role that the "new media" and newly important genres of the 1800s could have on a traveler. For example, though he could not see cinematic representations of the Castle d'If before reaching that famous prison, he makes it clear that reading popular novels by Dumas that included scenes set there colored completely his first direct encounter with the edifice. In addition, though he could not go on the web to preview his living-quarters abroad, he did read brochures and guidebooks that gave him clues about what to expect. And, as with the web, the information Twain gleaned from them turned out to be not so much inaccurate as incomplete. The digital photo of our Parisian apartment did not prepare us for the heady aroma that entered it whenever we opened a window, due to the apartment's proximity to a string of Egyptian, Greek, and Indian restaurants. Similarly, Twain was surprised that the guidebooks that sang the praises of the soaps of Marseilles did not tell him how hard it would be to find any bars of this substance with which to wash in that city's hotels.

Switching from sites and accommodations to famous works of

art, it is easy to imagine Twain feeling a kinship with the many contemporary travelers who wait in line in Paris to see the great Mona Lisa up close—then go away vaguely unsatisfied. Yes, these people say, it does look just like it does on the greeting cards and t-shirts. But it is hard to appreciate the famous smile when you come close to it, since the glass case encumbers your view. This postmodern disappointment echoes Twain's reaction to another Da Vinci work, *The Last Supper,* which he calls "the most celebrated painting in the world." When he saw *The Last Supper* he "recognized it in a moment," as it had served for centuries as the model for many "engravings" and "copies." "And, as usual," he continues, making a comment that he made as well about other renowned works, "I could not help noticing how superior the copies were to the original, that is, to my inexperienced eye." They were brighter and clearer, the details easier to make out.

———————

Still, one might suggest, there remain some dramatic contrasts between our day and Twain's. Yes, there may be contemporary counterparts to the know-it-alls of the 1860s that Twain lampoons, who would spout out, as though they were spontaneously formed opinions, impressive sounding comments on famous sites that turned out to be taken verbatim from a guidebook. The only difference is that now, the plagiarists often go to the Internet rather than printed matter for inspiration. But surely, one might argue, there was nothing around in Twain's time comparable to Epcot. To experience foreign travel then, you had to actually go abroad, did you not? Is it not only recently that going to an entertainment site allows one a literal and metaphoric taste of distant lands, a taste that can prepare you for an actual journey—or be substituted for an expensive and inconvenient undertaking? Can we not safely put Disney theme parks in a special category, reserved for contemporary simulations? The answer to all of these questions: no.

Consider, for example, the panoramas and dioramas of the 1800s. In 1824, one travel writer called panoramas "among the happiest contrivances for saving time and expense," since for a "shilling and a quarter of an hour" they allowed one to make a journey that once cost "a couple of hundred pounds." Sometimes, panoramas displayed events, such as battles, but sometimes they just represented locales. The same was true of dioramas. In 1845, for example, crowds flocked to a Parisian diorama devoted to simulating the experience of seeing St. Mark's in Venice. In short, as Schwartz puts it, panoramas and dioramas were early forms of " 'armchair' tourism" that might "substitute for travel." Such spectacles belonged to a milieu that included many other sorts of popular simulations that made a fetish of "realism," yet often included fanciful elements. Wax museums, for example, and the Paris Morgue, a site open to public viewing where bodies awaiting identification were placed on display, sometimes posed in dramatic ways or surrounded by props.

We do not know from Twain's account whether he saw any panoramas or dioramas or wax tableaus, either before or after heading across the Atlantic, that prepared him in advance for any particular sites.* We do know that, while in Paris, he joined the crowds outside the windows of the morgue. And, more significantly, he went to the 1867 International Exposition, also in Paris. The great international expositions and exhibitions of the nineteenth century—such as the Crystal Palace Exhibition of 1851 and its first American counterpart, the 1876 Centennial Exhibition held in Philadelphia—were precursors of the World's Fairs of the twentieth century. And these in turn would serve as models for the Disney theme parks.

Twain spent only two hours at the exposition—in part because he "saw at a glance that one would have to spend weeks—yea, even months—in that monstrous establishment, to get an intelligible idea of it." But he viewed his short time at the gala as a kind of miniaturized version of a world tour. The formal exhibits added up, he wrote, to a "wonderful show," allowing visitors to see objects from various

---

* This is in contrast to another famous traveler of the era who first crossed the Atlantic heading in the opposite direction: Thomas Cook. In 1873, in one of the missives that appeared in *Letters from the Sea and Foreign Lands,* Cook referred to his first overland trip across the United States spurring recollections of a "splendid panorama" he had seen "nearly 30 years" previously in Leicester that had included "scenes in the famous journey of John C. Fremont over the Prairies." This, he said, was one of the things that gave a sense of the "familiar" to his adventures in a distant country.

regions. And yet, he writes, "the moving masses of people of all nations" made "a still more wonderful show," and he closely examined the faces and modes of dress of those who passed by. It is perhaps no accident that one party he was especially fascinated by was made up of people who had come from the Middle East, the part of the world toward which he was headed.

Since rereading *Innocents Abroad,* I have been asking myself three different sets of "what if" questions about Twain's voyages across the globe and on the page. One set has to do with sites associated with him that show up on tourist itineraries. What would he make of Hannibal, Missouri, his boyhood home, becoming a heritage site? Would he be flattered, annoyed, or amused by Tom Sawyer's Island? And what would he say about the fact that the Magic Kingdom that now stands near Paris does *not* include this attraction? (Full disclosure: I am embarrassed to say that I have not yet made it to the European incarnation of Disneyland, so my information about it has been gleaned purely from a bit of armchair travel—done twenty-first-century style, of course, via the web.)

The second sort of "what if" questions I have been asking myself have to do with what Twain would have thought of Shanghai, the subject of my current research, had he visited there in the late 1800s. He had plans to go to China after completing his 1867 trip across the Atlantic, but despite an enduring interest in the country, he never made it.* I can thus only imagine—and this is frustrating for a Twain-loving Shanghai specialist—what he would have actually thought about the sights, sounds, and smells of China's leading treaty port in the late 1800s. Would he have thought that parts of the old walled city of Shanghai were strangely familiar when he arrived, due to his prior viewings of Chinese artifacts at international

---

* His interest in China showed through in many ways. There were his writing about American policies toward China and about treaties that affected treaty ports, for example. In addition, a character in one of his works of fiction sets off for America from Shanghai, and while in Hartford he befriended some of the first Chinese to come to the United States to study.

exhibitions or visits to one of America's Chinatowns? And if he had made it to Shanghai, would he have thought that the illustrations he had seen ahead of time of the new Western-style buildings of the famous waterfront esplanade, known as "The Bund," which ran through its newer foreign-run districts, had done them justice? There is, alas, no way to know for sure.

The final set of hypothetical questions I have been asking myself is what Twain's reaction would have been to certain experiences we had during our recent trip to France. I have decided that he would have liked our Parisian apartment, as the view from its window was a bit like a peephole into an international exposition. Looking out, we could see "people of all nations" pass by, as well as restaurants that not only served food from different countries but also had hosts or hostesses wearing the traditional clothing of and contained objects associated with those countries. One restaurant had a white statue of a Greek hero, another a sign saying "Visit Egypt" and a picture of the Pyramids. Our view was, in a sense, a window onto a miniature Epcot-on-the-Seine.

I think Twain would have been impressed by the speed with which we made the journey from Paris to Marseilles. In *Innocents Abroad*, Twain describes his preference for traveling by stagecoach rather than train, finding railway trips "tedious" and lacking in drama. Still, he was such an admirer of technological breakthroughs that he would have marveled that the TGV could whisk us from Paris to Marseilles in just a few hours. I am less sure what he would have thought of the precise fashion in which we made that journey. Though we had reserved seats, a strike leading to the cancellation of two-thirds of the southbound trains forced us into a small space usually reserved for luggage. Would he have found this a charming throwback to rough and ready travel by stagecoach? Interpreted it as a sign of the importance human factors will always have, no matter what technology accomplishes? Or simply lamented that we were deprived of seeing the landscape between Paris and Marseilles that he had found "bewitching"?

It is hard to decide what he would have thought about Nice, our final stop, which was not on his 1867 itinerary. Since Twain wrote a few revisionist accounts of Old Testament stories, it would be interesting to bring him back to life and ask his opinion of the representations of these tales in the Chagall Museum. And I would like to hear his comments, after a few days in Nice, on the ways that the clothes people wear at the seaside and the kinds of boats that ply the Mediterranean have changed since the 1860s. Most of all, though, if I could ask the author of *Innocents Abroad* about just one thing that we saw in Nice, it would be a restaurant-cum-nightclub called "Le Mississippi," which stands near the city's famed Hotel Negresco. From peeking into its window, my sense was that the main goal of the décor of Le Mississippi is to simulate for patrons the feeling of being on board a nineteenth-century American riverboat of the sort frequented and then made globally famous by Mark Twain. I would love to know the great man's reaction to this place, the French Riviera's glitzy answer to Disneyland's Tom Sawyer's Island.

Le Mississippi's existence intrigues me for another reason: it reminds us that cities throughout the world are now filled—much more so than in Twain's day—with sites that provide residents of other countries with simulated encounters with imagined Americas. It is worth keeping in mind that such simulacra—including, for example, the Hard Rock Cafés found everywhere from Beijing to Buenos Aires—can be powerful shapers of images. And it is worth considering, as I did in Nice, that such sites may seem just as exotic as additions to the local landscape as Epcot's faux Eiffel Tower is to that of Orlando.

7. Around the World with Grant and Li

Mark Twain was not the only famous Western globetrotter of the 1800s who never made it to Shanghai. The same was true, for example, of the best-known fictional European traveler of the day: Phileas Fogg, hero of Jules Verne's *Around the World in Eighty Days*. Fogg, like Twain, was planning to set foot on the Chinese mainland, but never got there. In Fogg's case, what happened was that, while en route from the island of Hong Kong to Shanghai, he found a way to shave some precious time off his itinerary by boarding a passing steamer bound for Japan.

Quite a few illustrious Westerners, on the other hand, did make it to Shanghai between the 1860s and 1890s, including Thomas Cook, a key figure in the invention of the modern tourist industry, and Andrew Carnegie.* And, interestingly, the most famous Westerner

---

* This was nothing, of course, compared to the 1920s and 1930s, the first period during which the city's status as a must-see destination for sophisticated globetrotters peaked, or the last decade or so, which has seen it regain this status. The long and

of all to visit Shanghai toward the end of the nineteenth century was a person who, albeit in very different ways, can be linked to both Twain and *Around the World in Eighty Days*. This was Ulysses S. Grant, who visited Shanghai after completing two terms as president of the United States—terms that had solidified and extended the global renown he had already gained due to his leadership of Union forces during the Civil War. Grant's link to Twain is well known: they were good friends. But what, the reader may wonder, is his connection to Verne's 1873 best-seller? A simple one, which attests to the degree of fame that Twain's friend enjoyed: *The General Grant* was the name that the French author gave to the ship that carried Fogg from Japan to San Francisco.

Grant's stop-over in Shanghai was in 1879, near the end of a round-the-world trip that lasted more than two years. The trip began early in 1877, and his departure point was Philadelphia—the same city in which he had met a Chinese traveler named Li Gui in August of the previous year. The ex-president's global circuit finally ended in San Francisco in September 1879, just after he completed a sea voyage that followed the same basic route as that Fogg took aboard *The General Grant* in Verne's novel. The general's trip included stays in many places that Twain had visited before him. One of these was Paris where, like the creator of Tom Sawyer and Huck Finn, Grant spent time at a Universal Exposition. But there were also major differences between their itineraries since Grant not only made it to China, which Twain never managed to do (though he eventually did get to India in the 1890s), but also to Japan, another country that the writer never visited. Another significant contrast between Grant's trip and the one that Twain wrote about in *Innocents Abroad,* besides the fact that it took longer and involved a full

---

varied list of celebrated foreigners who stopped in the treaty port early in the twentieth century included Albert Einstein, Margot Fonteyn, Christopher Isherwood, W. H. Auden, Noel Coward, and the future Duchess of Windsor, Wallace Simpson. An equally long and varied list could be compiled of celebrated foreigners who have recently visited Shanghai, ranging from Hollywood actors who have gone there to shoot scenes from films (Tom Cruise) or to help publicize the Chinese premiere of one of their movies (Meryl Streep), to Mick Jagger and Keith Richard (who led the Rolling Stones there in 2006 for the band's first concert on the Chinese mainland).

circumnavigation of the globe and stops in East Asia, has to do with the kinds of receptions that greeted the ex-president in various ports of call. Grant's military exploits and years as president guaranteed him, as Twain's just-budding reputation as a writer did not, lavish ceremonies of welcome in many places. And Shanghai was no exception.

One of the best places to find details concerning these Shanghai ceremonies is *Around the World with General Grant,* a book by journalist John Russell Young (incidentally, also a friend of Twain's) that first came out in 1879 and is now back in print as a 2002 Johns Hopkins University Press reissue. It is a treasure trove of information for anyone who, like me, is interested in China's past and the history of travel. But what made it a best-seller was something different: Young's savvy decision to combine descriptions of exotic places with renditions of conversations he had with the general en route about the best-known people and battles associated with the Civil War.

What, then, does Young tell us about Shanghai? He notes that when Grant reached the city, an enormous crowd of local Chinese, "at least one hundred thousand" strong, "lined the banks" of the river to greet their ship. And upon entering the treaty port, the scene as the visitors "drove out into the open street was bewildering in its beauty," thanks to the efforts to which different national groups, including not just local American, French, and British residents but also Japanese consular officials and businessmen, went to make the general's first impressions of Shanghai memorable. In addition to fireworks and massive "gas jet" displays that the main English language local newspaper insisted were the most impressive ever mounted in the city, enormous numbers of lanterns were used to spell out phrases of welcome and praise, such as "Washington, Lincoln, Grant—three immortal Americans."

By one of the odd processes through which information about China can filter into and circulate through the West, the section of Young's book devoted to Grant's stay in Shanghai doubtless provided quite a few American Civil War buffs of the late 1800s with their first details about the treaty port. This is because, given Young's method, even if they were uninterested in East Asia, they could not afford to skip a chapter just because it had a name like "On to

China," the title of the one that deals with Shanghai. Why? Because these often provided comments in passing about the Civil War. Just before describing the party's Shanghai stay, in fact, come several paragraphs on what Grant said while they were "steaming along the Chinese coasts" and able to "resume the conversations" about the 1860s that formed "so pleasant a feature in our journey."

There was something risky as well as shrewd about Young's decision to intersperse accounts of conversational journeys back in time to the days of Abraham Lincoln and Robert E. Lee with accounts of the group's journey through distant lands, as Michael Fellman notes in his introduction to the Johns Hopkins reissue of *Around the World with General Grant*. The risk was that the general would someday write his memoirs, and in doing so strip Young's travelogue-mixed-with-reminiscences of much of its allure. And this is just what happened. In the early 1880s, Grant set about writing two volumes of memoirs, which were published with the help of his friend Mark Twain, one of those who realized that writing about his Civil War experiences (the main focus of the volumes) was the general's best strategy for digging himself out of what by then was a deep financial hole. Twain may have gone too far in praising Grant's account of his military career (he said it was the best work of its kind by a general since Julius Caesar's foray into the genre), but the former president's memoirs were generally well-received. And it is not surprising that most Civil War buffs, past and present, have preferred reading General Grant's own written descriptions of the battle charges he led, rivals who challenged him, and comrades who fought beside him to reading Young's accounts of shipboard conversations about those same events and people.

––––––––––

Personally, though, I find *Around the World with General Grant* by far the more interesting work, since his time in China intrigues me more than his time on the battlefield, and the ex-president's memoirs essentially stop with the end of the Civil War. Young's book, by contrast, while it pays plenty of attention to battles even in chapters with China in their titles, has much to say about several different Chinese cities. Perhaps most interestingly of all, it also tells us what, at least according to Young, the general thought of China's future prospects. And reading these sections of *Around the World with General Grant* early in the twenty-first-century, there are more than a few things that resonate with contemporary commentaries on where China might be headed.

This is intriguing because the country that Grant visited was so very different from the China of today. It was a land that had been laid low by a series of military and diplomatic defeats, beginning with the Opium War of 1839–1842. And it was a land that had been rocked by domestic upheavals such as the great millenarian Taiping Uprising of 1850–1864, which was led by a charismatic prophet, Hong Xiuquan, who claimed to be the younger brother of Jesus Christ. Defeat at the hands of the West had transformed Hong Kong into a British colony and Shanghai into one of several partially colonized treaty-port cities, which were divided into Chinese-run districts and foreign-run enclaves. The domestic upheavals, meanwhile, had drained the imperial treasuries and been accompanied by enormous death tolls (that of the Taipings alone far exceeded that of the American Civil War). And yet, despite all this, the general was bullish on China's prospects—bullish in a way that is reflected in the present.

Grant thought it very likely that, if the country could find a way to take full advantage of new technologies, it would rise to prominence. China was "not a military power," but had "all the elements of a strong, great, and independent empire, and may, before many years roll around, assert their power." The "leading men of China" with whom he conversed, Grant claimed, seemed determined to "gradually educate a sufficient number of their own people to fill all places of development of railroads, manufactories, telegraphs, and all those elements of civilization so new to them but common and even old to us." Grant would not be surprised, if he heard "within the next twenty years, if I should live so long, more complaints of Chinese absorption of the trade and commerce of the world than we hear now of their backward position."

The general noted, though, that for this economic transformation to occur, a "marked political change" would need to take place in China. The Qing Dynasty (1644–1911) would need to fall or at least alter dramatically the outdated way in which it operated. This was needed, presumably, so that obstacles were removed from the paths of the "leading men" Grant met, such as a famous statesman and general named Li Hongzhang—no relationship to the Li Gui that Grant met in Philadelphia, though, as we will see below, the two Lis were connected to one another via first an institution and then later a text. People like Li Hongzhang, an influential figure among "Self-Strengtheners" (those advocating swifter and more widespread adoption of foreign institutions and technologies than more conservative elements within the elite) and someone with whom Grant formed a close tie during his visit, struck the former president as appealingly pragmatic and no-nonsense types. The way he responded to Li Hongzhang, who had played a key role in the suppression of the Taiping Uprising, was not so very different from the way that some much later American leaders responded to Deng Xiaoping. And it is no mere coincidence that while the Self-Strengtheners were reviled by the Communists at some earlier points (due in part to Mao Zedong celebrating the Taipings as proto-socialists who had practiced a progressive sort of land reform, in part to Chiang Kai-shek identifying his own anti-Communist crusade with the anti-Taiping fight of Li Hongzhang and his mentor Zeng Guofan), they began to be treated as farsighted patriots in the Deng Xiaoping era and continue to be treated that way in China's post-Deng era (1997–).

There is another reason, though, unrelated to China, why *Around the World with General Grant* appeals to me more than the ex-president's memoirs. Namely, as already shown in the previous chapter, I am intrigued by how a traveler's view of a place can be influenced by previous exposure to representations of that locale, and Young gives us something fascinating to ponder in this regard. "My friend Mark Twain will be glad to know," he writes, "that the General read with delight and appreciation his 'Innocents Abroad'"— just before, though Young does not note this, their traveling party visited some of the exact same sites described reverently or irreverently in that book.

Still, as engaging as Young's travelogue is to someone with my interests, in one way it has proven just as frustrating a text as the general's memoirs. This is because it has nothing to say about the Philadelphia Centennial Exhibition of 1876. There are several things that I would like to know about Grant's time at that first World's Fair held in the United States, but about these Young provides no illumination.

I am very curious, for example, about whether Grant visited the Chinese display, which was provided to the Fair by an unusual organization known as the Imperial Chinese Maritime Customs Service. What made this organization so unusual was that, though its purpose was to ensure that China's government received appropriate duties, its top officials by the 1870s were mostly foreign employees of the Qing Dynasty, and it was run by an Ulsterman named Robert Hart. One of the best descriptions of the Chinese exhibit the Customs Service provided can be found in an 1876 National Publishing Company commemorative album, *The Illustrated History of the Centennial Exhibition.* According to this text, a visit to the Chinese pavilion in Philadelphia was seen by some as the next best thing to an actual trip to China. Not only did visitors get to see "rich, valuable, and exceedingly interesting" Chinese objects, including "tall pagodas and towers ornamented with the most brilliant colors," but also people from China "in their native costumes." The cumulative effect was such, according to the *Illustrated History,* that you could "for a moment imagine that you had put the sea between you and the Exhibition and had suddenly landed in some large Chinese bazaar." Reading the *Illustrated History* makes me keen to know whether, if Grant saw the display, as seems likely, he was reminded of it when he set foot in an actual "Chinese bazaar" three years later. Alas, we may never know, as Young does not mention Grant seeing the exhibit in 1876 or thinking about it in 1879.

What especially frustrates me about the fact that neither Young's book nor the general's memoirs deal with the then-president's visits to the Centennial Exhibition is that this means that I am left with only Li Gui's own account of what transpired when he met Grant in Philadelphia—and that account is skimpy, to say the least. We know a great deal about why Li Gui took his trip around the world (the main reason was to spend time as an observer at the Centennial Exhibition, taking notes on it for the Customs Service, for which he worked), what he did before he reached Philadelphia (his route there began in Shanghai, passed through Japan, and continued on through San Francisco), and where his travels took him after leaving the World's Fair (through Europe and the Suez canal and then back to Shanghai via Southeast Asia and then Hong Kong).

We know all of this, as well as details about what he thought of many of the people he met and places he saw during his trip, since Li Gui wrote a book about his experiences that makes particularly interesting reading when placed beside Young's *Around the World with General Grant*. Li's book, *Huan you diqiu xin lu* (A new account of a trip around the globe) was published in Shanghai in 1878, with a foreword by Li Hongzhang that helped it gain the attention of reform-minded members of the Chinese elite. In 2004, it became available for the first time in a full-length English language version, when the University of Michigan Press published a translation by Charles Desnoyers as *A Journey to the East*.

In addition to what we can learn about many aspects of Li Gui's travels, it is also easy to discover facts about his life before and after his trip abroad, thanks to Chinese sources and the very useful introduction that Desnoyers provides to *A Journey to the East*. But Li's encounter with Grant is not dealt with at any length in the main text of *A Journey to the East,* nor something about which Desnoyers has much to say in his notes and introductory section. For his part, Li merely mentions that on such and such a day, he attended a reception, along with various others (including a group of Chinese students studying in the United States who had come on a visit to the Centennial Exhibition), and met the president.

If the historian, as Henry James put it in his introduction to *The Aspern Papers,* "wants more documents than he can really use," while the "dramatist only wants more liberties than he can really take," this is one of those cases in which it would be much better to be a dramatist than a historian. Writing as a historian, all I can say about the meeting is that we do not know what Li and Grant said to one another (if anything) nor what they made of each other. If I were a dramatist, on the other hand, this meeting would be rich with possibilities, for there is so much that the two men had in common and could have talked about, had they realized this fact.

What then might they have said, had they had the time and inclination? By 1876, with the end of his presidency in sight, Grant might already have been contemplating a world tour of the sort that Li was midway through, so it is easy to imagine Grant asking Li for suggestions about where to spend time when he got to the China leg of his trip. Since Li began and would eventually end his own journey in Shanghai, had this subject come up, it seems likely that he would have stressed to Grant the importance of including that port on his itinerary. But as a native of a village not far from Nanjing, he might have tried to convince Grant to head up the Yangzi toward that famed city as well. (Though perhaps not, as Nanjing had just been through one of the rougher periods in its history, due to having been conquered by the Taipings, who used it as their capital before the city was retaken by the forces mustered to suppress the uprisings.) And since Li Gui worked in Ningbo, a port near Shanghai, he might have put in a plug for Grant to stop there, too. In addition, if, as seems likely, Grant had seen the Chinese exhibit at the World's Fair, he might well have asked Li Gui whether he thought this creation of his employers accurately conveyed a sense of his country.

Travel and the Chinese exhibit, though two obvious topics for conversation between the two men, would not be the only ones, for wartime experiences would be another common subject. After all, as we learn from Desnoyers, though Li Gui was no general, he, like Grant, had been affected greatly by battles that took place during a mid-nineteenth-century civil war. This is because, during the Taiping Uprising, a teenaged Li and many of his relatives were taken captive by the insurgents. Most of his kinsmen were killed by the Taipings, but Li Gui was spared. This was because he was being trained to take the examinations to become a government official. Hence his writing skills were good enough that the Taipings decided he was worth more to them alive than dead and put him to work keeping records and writing messages for them.

After a few years, he managed to escape, and initially took up a post as a secretary for a joint Chinese-foreign military enterprise, the "Ever Victorious Army," a group whose main goal was to defeat the

Taipings and which counted among its leaders Li Hongzhang—the other Li who, as noted above, would later befriend General Grant and do Li Gui the favor of writing an appreciative foreword for *A Journey to the East*. According to Desnoyers, it was probably through contacts that Li Gui made in this post that he secured his position in "a more ambitious and, ultimately, longer-lived Sino-foreign venture," the Imperial Maritime Customs Service. Like Grant, moreover, Li eventually wrote a memoir that focused on his wartime experiences, *Sitong ji* (Bitter memories), which Desnoyers calls a "searing" account of a brutally violent period. Neither the president nor the customs employee had yet written their memoirs in 1876, though, so those could not have been a topic of conversation, unless a dramatist were to assume that each was already contemplating his memoirs-to-be.

In the end, there might be so much that a dramatist as opposed to a historian would want to do with Li and Grant that limiting their contact to a single meeting, even one with a lot of conversation, would begin to feel too constricting. Why not, one might wonder, take a very big liberty, while still remaining within the realm of the possible if not the provable nor even the probable, and imagine that Grant and Li saw each other a second time, when the general stopped in Shanghai? Li Gui was back in China by then and working nearby in Ningbo, so there is no reason why it could not have happened, even if there is not a single shred of evidence to suggest that it did.

A dramatist imagining the dialogue for such a reunion on the other side of the world from Philadelphia could have a field day, as there would be so many things for the two men to talk about. Even though Grant would have only recently come to China by that point, with his stay in Beijing still lying in the future, his vision of the country's future prospects might have begun to form, and he might have shared them with Li. If so, he would have found a man who agreed with many of his basic premises. For example, one of the reasons that Li Gui wrote—and Li Hongzhang endorsed—*A Journey to the East* was to support the Self-Strengthening position by providing details about Western machinery and institutions of a sort that would encourage readers to view them positively. Thus the book, though far from uncritical of the West in other regards (the United States is taken to task by Li Gui, for example, for its treatment of Chinese immigrants), is filled with admiring discussions of new modes of conveyance (including the railroads that Grant thought so crucial for China to adopt), new technologies of communication (such as telegraph systems), and new kinds of weaponry (including the massive German canons that were displayed at the Centennial Exhibition, as they were at other World's Fairs of the time). And in his section on Japan, Li Gui applauds, as Young says Grant would in 1879, the use to which Western technologies were being put there.

It is interesting to contemplate one more topic that Grant and Li might have talked about in Shanghai, one on which their opinions would likely have varied greatly, if we base our speculations on what we learn from *Around the World with General Grant* and *A Journey to the East*. Namely, what made Europe interesting to visit. Grant, though not one to be terribly impressed by ruins and old paintings and so forth, seems to have felt, like many Americans of the time, including Twain, that Europe's interest lay in the window it opened onto the past. Li Gui, by contrast, whose only European stops were Britain and France, had a different view of the continent. He seems to have been quite taken with some of the older things he saw, thinking Notre Dame "magnificent," for example. But what drew his attention most, as had been true in America, were technological marvels he encountered in Europe, such as the General Telegraph Office in London that contained wonders such as a "small box" that had wires that could send message instantly "to the major cities in all the different countries of the globe," and a British armory where there were "fifty machines for manufacturing small arms ammunition" that could each "make sixty thousand bullets per day."

Thinking about this contrast, it begins to make sense that Young incorporated so much more reflection on historical events into his account. The general's party thought of themselves as moving through lands that were in some ways most notable for what their inhabitants had done in the past. But Li was most concerned, for understandable reasons, with using his time abroad to learn things that, when conveyed to his countrymen, could help them improve China's chances of surviving in an unsettling present and a future in which new technologies seemed certain to play crucial roles.

8. The Time Machine of Tippecanoe County

When I was a child, *Time Tunnel* was one of my favorite television shows. Each week, the main characters would journey to a different moment in the past and have to perform some task that would ensure that history unfolded in the proper fashion. Even when I was young, the plots often struck me as contrived and the special effects—including the swirling shapes of the "tunnel" that took the heroes backward in time—seemed hokey and cheap. Still, I was drawn to the show by the invitation to imagine what it was like in a different era. I have wondered sometimes whether television programs and movies like that one (there were others with similar themes) helped push me toward a career teaching and writing about the past, or whether it was a sensibility that led me toward history that also made me like those kinds of entertainments.

In any case, I sometimes find myself thinking about *Time Tunnel* at odd times and in curious places. During a 2002 trip to Shanghai, for example, I thought about the show's cheesy special effects the first time I ventured into the "Bund Sightseeing Tunnel," which carries visitors under the Huangpu River in a strange vehicle reminiscent of the People Mover ride at Disneyland, bombarding them while in transit with a psychedelic light display. And I thought about the movement-between-eras aspect of the show at different points during that same trip, such as when I saw people dressed up to look like servants of China's pre-1911 imperial era waiting outside a Starbucks in the oldest section of Shanghai, holding onto the carrying poles of a palanquin or sedan chair, hoping that tourists making their way through the biggest city in revolutionary China would hire them to ride for a time in the style of pre-revolutionary elites.

Closer to home, while I lived in Indiana (from mid-1991 through mid-2006), I thought about *Time Tunnel* each time I went to the "Feast of the Hunters' Moon," an annual two-day festival that, for more than thirty years, has been held in the northern part of the state, in Lafayette, a city best known as the home of Purdue University. Sponsored by the Tippecanoe County Historical Association, this October gathering is a popular one. According to the local newspaper the 1998 Feast drew more than 60,000 visitors—though crowds are considerably smaller when the weather is unusually cool and damp. Some visitors are from the immediate area but others drive for an hour or two to take part in it, as my family did several times when we lived in Bloomington.

What exactly made us willing to make the journey, and to not only pay the price of admission ($8 for adults, $3 for children circa 2000) but also the added cost of purchasing food and souvenirs at often over-priced booths? One attraction of the event is the same attraction that *Time Tunnel* had: it offers visitors the opportunity to watch groups of people clothed in eighteenth-century garb re-enact historical (or, rather, legendary) events from the time when Lafayette was a frontier trading post known as Ouiatenon. When we went, we also got to listen to music played by groups of folk musicians on make-shift stages, while consuming unusual food items (such as rabbit stew) and drinking more ordinary beverages (such as hot apple cider). And, if we were so inclined, we could buy various things to take home to remind us of the past—or simply of the fair. These ranged from woven baskets and other goods produced by costumed craftspeople to books on historical themes

(John Keegan's *Warpaths: Travels of a Military Historian in North America* was among those offered for sale). It was the lure of this mixture of attractions, as well as our fondness for spending time with friends who live in the area, that brought my family to the fair several times, including a memorable soggy Sunday in October of 1999, our third visit.

To aid seasoned Feast-goers, which we were by that time, as well as novices, a brochure was provided at the gate that day that described the fair's special events and clarified its meaning. It informed us that "the Feast generates at least $1.5 million in visitor spending" in the area. "Food booths," the same brochure also noted, "provided hungry visitors" with well over 3,000 pounds of buffalo meat and 5,000 pounds of chicken in the busy year of 1998. The general aim of the gathering, it noted, is to recreate the feeling of that "time 250 years ago when the bountiful harvests and the arrival of the fur trade canoes were joyously celebrated by the French habitants and the Native people with singing, dancing, and merriment." The event's goal, it claimed, was to remind us of "the integral link that existed between humans and their environment at Ouiatenon in the 18th century." Environmental as well as multicultural lessons were, apparently, there for the learning.

Thinking about this vision of the Feast (as an event that celebrates "the circle of life" and the mixing of cultural influences) and looking around at the thousand or so people dressed up in costumes of various sorts who had gathered at the fairgrounds that October, I was struck by a realization. The gathering was, in many ways, both a quintessentially 1990s experience and a decidedly American heritage experience. It was not just that the past being commemorated was that of the United States, but also that the activities involved combined in creative ways and gave local twists to elements of what were by that point the two main autumn celebrations for many Americans: Thanksgiving and Halloween.

Like Thanksgiving, the fair is a feast day linked to a perception of the centuries following 1492 as ones in which people from different backgrounds discovered new ways to cooperate with one another and lived in harmony with nature. The European settlers may, in the case of the Feast of the Hunters' Moon, be French traders as opposed to Pilgrims, but the use of melting pot imagery to expiate the original sin of conquest is the same.

The similarities with Halloween were just as easy to see. A central part of the Feast, after all, is watching people dressed up in unusual and sometimes outlandish clothing. Going from place to place in search of edible treats is also a central activity. Again, there are differences, of course. Namely, it is not mainly children who wear the costumes and do the eating here. In addition, only some of the food involved is sweet; for every booth selling sugary fried dough confections, there is another offering savories like sausage on a stick. Still, a Halloween meets Thanksgiving vision of the Feast captures the feel of the event pretty well, though there is also a bit of historical theme park and open air museum thrown in.

One thing that struck me on that third visit (and would again on later ones) was that each annual incarnation of the Feast is both reassuringly similar to and just a bit different from the preceding one. The parades of fife and drum corps always look the same, but there have been novel food items to sample each year. There have also always been new types of re-enacters' costumes to marvel at and previously unrepresented (or perhaps just previously unnoticed by us) old-time crafts for our children to try their hands at—in 1999 it was candle-making.

More generally, changes are continually rung on the enduring themes of environmentalism and multiculturalism. The reference to the "circle of life" on the 1999 brochure, for example, was doubtless a recent addition, which paid homage to the most famous song from a then-recent Disney film, *The Lion King*. That novel wrinkles are frequently being added to melting pot narratives is probably inevitable in contexts such as this, given the protean and charged nature of multiculturalism within the American political and social landscape these days.

This brings me to the most bizarre and interesting moment in the 1999 Feast, which took place in the section of the fairgrounds devoted to Native American traditions. According to the always handy brochure, the performance in question was the work of a group called the "Spirit Wind Singers and Dancers," all of whom claim descent from indigenous peoples of the area. The leader of the group wore the expected feathered headdress but what he held in his hand was a less expected piece of equipment—a cordless microphone.

It was, however, not the microphone itself but the things he said through it during his alternately engaging and disquieting monologue that gave this particular performance a surreal quality. He began by saying that his job was to explain to the gathered crowd—about one hundred people who stood around in a wide ring, while musicians and dancers played drums and moved to the music in a central grassy area—some things about Native Americans. His manner was reminiscent at first of a patient schoolteacher, but sometimes he slid into one more like that of a Las Vegas nightclub host.

One of the first things he did was ask the audience if everyone was having fun. He then cajoled those of us standing on one side of the ring for being less enthusiastic in responding to his question than were those on the other. He next called on members of the audience to step into the ring and join the dance in progress, insisting that if they did so, they would feel better for it, as merely participating in the "spirit dances" developed by his ancestors could have physically and spiritually restorative powers.

He insisted throughout that his desire was to debunk some common misunderstandings we were likely to have about Native Americans and encourage us to view all people as equal and worthy of respect. "Many of you probably still think we need to kill an animal to eat," he said at one point, "but actually the only place most Native Americans go hunting these days is in the supermarket." The contemporary descendants of indigenous peoples, he stressed, now spend a lot more time eating pizza than buffalo meat.

This de-exoticizing of Native Americans was amusing and in its own way maybe even useful in undermining enduring prejudices. The final part of his commentary, however, was strangely disturbing, at least to me, in the way it treated racial differences as linked in simple, timeless, natural ways to skin color. This is, unfortunately, still a commonly accepted idea in the United States, which plays into the hands of bigots and hate groups—hence the disquiet I felt. What he said was that we should all note the four colors woven into his clothing: red, white, black, and yellow. These had always represented to his people the four races of the world, the speaker continued. We should, he said, learn from the way the four colors were woven together into the fabric, since this was how the Great Spirit had always taught his people things should be. All four races were different, but each was of equal value, and they were meant to live side by side in harmony, not to fight one another.

Heritage events such as the Feast of the Hunters' Moon are supposed to allow and indeed encourage visitors to travel back in time in their minds, to imagine what life was like in periods that are part of the distant past. With this monologue and the brochure's reference to the "circle of life" filling my mind, however, I left that particular incarnation of the Feast with different kinds of thoughts about the past. I found myself less interested in trying to conjure up how life was lived in the Tippecanoe area in the 1700s than with thinking about how the relationship between cultures and between humans and their environment were discussed when the first of these annual gatherings was held in the 1960s. Surely, they were handled very differently then in the days before *The Lion King* and cordless mics, though I would love to know just how so. The stars of *Time Tunnel* would have an easy method for figuring this out, but without the right apparatus at hand and an event that falls below the radar of the sort of record-keeping on which historians typically depend, it is difficult to know how to proceed.

PART THREE

TURN-OF-THE-CENTURY

FLASHBACKS

Protest posters displayed at Beijing University, May 9, 1999. Slogans in Chinese include "Down with American Imperialism" and "Long Live the People of China." *Photograph by the author.*

9. Mixed Emotions: China in 1999

"Were you scared?"

People kept asking me this when I got back from a trip I took to China in 1999. The question didn't surprise me. After all, while I was in Beijing and then Shanghai a series of anti-American demonstrations (triggered by NATO bombs which hit the Chinese Embassy in Belgrade on May 7 during a campaign to halt atrocities in Kosovo, bombs that killed three PRC journalists) had broken out. The people who asked me whether I had been afraid had read reports of Westerners in general and Americans in particular being taunted and sworn at by outraged Chinese citizens. They had heard about foreign journalists being handled roughly by crowds, seen photos of the ambassador trapped inside the American Embassy in Beijing, and watched televised footage of the burning of the U.S. consulate in Chengdu. Some may even have come across sensationalist news reports that compared the anti-American demonstrations (during which no one was seriously injured, let alone killed) to the attacks on foreigners that accompanied the Boxer Uprising of

1899–1900, a violent insurrection that continues to loom large in U.S. popular images of China thanks to revisitations of it in everything from a Cold War–era epic starring Charlton Heston (*55 Days at Peking*) to a flashback episode of the cult television show *Buffy the Vampire Slayer* set in Beijing at the turn of the twentieth century.

One reason people were curious about my degree of fear was that they knew something about my movements while in China. They were aware that not only had I been in the PRC at a dramatic moment, but that at times I had been in particular places that were at or near the heart of the demonstrations. They knew from e-mails I had sent home, for example, that I had spent the evening of May 9 wandering through the legation quarter of Beijing with some other academic China specialists (ironically, we had all come to attend a conference held to mark the anniversary of the May 4th Movement, the famous anti-imperialist struggle of 1919) and a couple of foreign journalists. And that I had spent much of the following week hanging around alone on Shanghai campuses—key locales because, during the 1999 protests (like those of the 1980s but very unlike the Boxer Uprising carried out by villagers), students had played central roles.

Even though I expected the question, even though the people who asked had good reason to wonder whether I felt fear, and even though at points I certainly felt afraid while in China that spring, the query always took me aback. The reason was that, while I was definitely scared sometimes—like when I was a few feet away from people throwing rocks at the British Embassy and paint balls at the American one less than 48 hours after the three Chinese journalists were killed in Belgrade—many emotions other than fear (from amusement to frustration to sadness to relief) were part of my experience in Beijing and Shanghai that week. It seemed to distort and belittle the meaning of the moment to boil it all down to: "Were you scared?"

This is more than just a personal point. Many Western journalists (the two I hung out with in Beijing being among the exceptions) presented Chinese outrage (often described as exaggerated) and American fear (often described as totally justified) as together constituting *the* story of those strange and interesting days—when, for

Chinese student protesters in Beijing, near the American Embassy, May 9, 1999. Note the image of the American Eagle encircling the globe to the right, and the image of the American Eagle with feathers shaped like missiles to the left. *Photograph by David Kenley, used by permission.*

many people, there was much more to it than that. All the complexity and confusion of the time was reduced to a simple plot line, and things that did not make for good soundbites or dramatic photos, as so often happens, were left out of the story. Just how this dynamic can work came home to me with a jolt on the morning of May 10, when I stood in downtown Beijing on a street corner near the embassies. I had just finished doing a television interview, which was later shown on Australian and British public television, that focused on my reaction to the protests as a specialist in the history of Chinese student movements. I was trying to hail a cab to take me to the airport to catch a plane down to Shanghai to do some research on recent changes in that city, which was one of the things that had brought me across the Pacific. A reporter from the Hong Kong–based *South China Morning Post,* seeing me with my suitcases in hand and thinking my voice sounded American, ran up excitedly to ask if I was fleeing the demonstrators and heading back to the States. When I told her what I was actually doing, she sighed, then dashed off to find the kind of person she needed a quote from to add color to her story, doubtless already written in her head, about the fear being generated by the movement.

If fear wasn't what I mainly felt, what kinds of emotions jostled with it for pride of place during the days I tracked the protests? Well, there was plenty of amusement—in part because some very good jokes about Li Peng, the least liked of China's top leaders at the time, were making the rounds on Shanghai campuses the week I spent there. There was also sadness—due to both the deaths caused by the U.S. bombs and the juvenile nastiness of some of the posters reviling Americans in the nastiest of possible terms that showed up on campus walls. There was as well, at certain moments, a sense of disappointment. It was disappointing at a personal level to learn, for example, from an article in *Salon* pulled off the web in Shanghai's "Internet Bar" (one of the places Bill Clinton visited on his 1998 trip to China), that when I had been in Beijing, I had just missed getting to meet the rocker Cui Jian, China's answer to Bruce Springsteen and an inspirational figure to the protesters of 1989. He had come to Beijing University to read the wall posters at almost, but not quite, the same time that I had been checking them out.

There were other minor disappointments, including the fact that the 1999 protests were so much less theatrically satisfying than those of 1989. The musical soundtrack for this movement was, in a word, boring. In 1989, students sang everything from Cui Jian's rousing "Nothing to My Name," to the "The Internationale," to the folk-tinged "Children of the Dragon" (by Taiwan folk singer Hou Dejian who joined the protesters at Tiananmen Square). This time, how-ever, the repertoire was limited almost exclusively to the Chinese na-tional anthem. The visual dimensions of the protests were a bit more creative, including some intriguing caricatures of stupid or evil-looking Americans on banners and a fascinating picture of an American eagle, each of whose feathers was a missile. Even here, though, there was less to marvel at than there had been when watch-ing the televised footage of the 1989 protests that preceded the June 4th Massacre.

Yet another emotion more prevalent than fear even on the evening of May 9, at least within the group I was part of, can best be de-scribed as giddiness. It was exciting for people like us who teach or write about China for a living to be able to watch history being made—and one thing that was clear was that, for better or worse, the Belgrade bombing and the protests would go down as some kind of historical turning point. Especially intriguing was the appearance of so many tactics and slogans from the recent and distant past. For example, calls for a boycott of foreign goods had been heard at least once a decade during the protest movements of the first half of the last century, including during the May 4th Movement, and here they were again. The slogan "Resist America/Support Yugoslavia," meanwhile, was a direct variation on the "Resist America/Support Korea" campaign that the CCP had promoted in the early 1950s.

It became a game of sorts to see how many historical precedents we could find. The protests of 1999 were not just like any past event, and some of the images were distinctively part of this mo-ment. The omnipresent "target" symbol borrowed from Belgrade's anti-NATO demonstrations is one example, images of the Statue of Liberty with a swastika on her face or blood on her hands are others. The echoes of the past were, however, an important part of the cacophony around us. Another source of giddiness came from knowing that, whatever else this disturbing event was, it was definitely one that would help define the political identity of a generation of Chinese students.

Annoyance was still another feeling more common than fear. One source of annoyance was the misrepresentation of the protests by the PRC media (which downplayed the anti-foreign violence and erroneously described the demonstrations as completely spontaneous, when official organizations had provided transportation and food to students involved in the demonstrations). But another was the misleading line typically staked out by the Western press, which distorted things in the opposite way. American reports often expressed skepticism that there was any genuineness to the anger of the youths, when clearly there was plenty of understandable outrage at what had happened—hardly surprising since it is bound to be disturbing to people when bombs hit one of their country's embassies.

Despite all these mixed emotions, it was certainly tempting to pretend, when I returned to the States, that fear was the key one, since this would have allowed me to make my tale a dramatic and self-serving one. The temptation grew especially great when I learned that Arnold Schwarzenegger, then still known purely as an actor rather than an actor-turned-politician, had decided to postpone his trip to China. It would have been fun to turn my story of being in Beijing and Shanghai into a tale of risk-taking and daring do—perhaps working up a written account of it titled "To Boldly Go (Where the Terminator Feared to Tread)." I could dwell on members of the group I was part of on May 9 being sworn at and spit upon in Beijing ("Are you Americans?" a man shouted at us from across the street in Chinese at one point, "If you are I'd like to kill you!"), and the sense of defying an authoritarian state that came from nervously scurrying from campus to campus to take pictures of wall posters the following week in Shanghai. I could also turn into a tale straight out of a spy novel some of my meetings with old and newly made Chinese friends. I would hand them rolled up copies of the *International Herald Tribune* I had bought at foreign-run hotels, and they would pass on information about a march or a wall poster. One even gave me copies of photos she had taken of the posters that had appeared on the walls of her Shanghai campus on May 9, when I was in Beijing. These had been much more virulent than those I had gotten to see in Shanghai. She wanted me to know that, even in cosmopolitan Shanghai, students had been "passionate" enough in their initial rage to write out slogans such as (in English) "FUCK CLINTON, FUCK NATO, FUCK GRE, FUCK TOEFL." In exchange, I told her about the one at Beijing University I had seen that called Clinton a "biraper," who had first ravished Monica and was now out to rape the whole world.

The fact is, however, that even though the incidents just mentioned did occur, there is a more accurate or at least to my mind more revealing tale to tell about my time in China on May 9 and the days that followed, in which fear is relegated to a very minor part. And in the late 1990s—when some pundits and politicians were inaccurately presenting China as an unchanging totalitarian state and when many Americans had overly simplistic notions about what had just taken place there—that more complex story seemed important to convey. At the present moment, when there is a post-9/11 tendency within the United States to think of anything that one can call "anti-Americanism" as a single terrifying thing and talk of a menacing "China Threat" is once again being heard in some quarters, it may again be particularly important to try to tell that more complicated tale.

What is this other version of the story of being an American in China in May of 1999? It is one in which it can be acknowledged, as it could not in the version that focused on bravery, that the only time I got hassled by a policeman was when I tried to enter the beautiful new Shanghai public library wearing sandals instead of shoes. It is also one in which it can be pointed out that the Chinese person I heard raise her voice highest in a one-on-one conversation with me was not a protester but a woman who worked for a tour company. She, like all the Chinese I met, was outraged, understandably, by the bombing of the Belgrade embassy. She was sure that it had been no mere accident, that there was more to the event than the story of outdated maps that the U.S. government was sticking to. None of this, however, was what made her shout. Instead, what inspired her to yell was the fact that the anti-American protests were likely to cause a fall-off in U.S. tourist bookings, which had only recently recovered fully from the damage done by the bloodshed of 1989.

The alternative version of events I have in mind is one in which it can be noted as well that no one seemed to care that I was taking pictures of wall posters on campuses. Nor did the police outside of the American consulate in Shanghai mind when I took photographs of them. I *was* stopped, however, when I tried to use my camera inside a KFC outlet, hoping to get some shots of Chinese customers buying fried chicken to pass on to a colleague working on Colonel Sanders as a global symbol and the international political economy of fast food franchises.

Perhaps the best way to frame this more complicated story is simply to take up one by one three emotions other than fear that became associated for me with the aftermath of the "May 8th Tragedy"—to use the term for the bombing that became common in China, due to the day, Beijing time, that the three PRC journalists in Belgrade were killed. This is what I will do here, arranging the feelings—frustration, relief, amusement—in no particular order.

Frustration

One recurrent source of frustration was, as already noted, the way the Chinese media handled the events. It was upsetting to learn, through e-mails and phone calls to the United States and by surfing the web and reading international newspapers, that Clinton and others had apologized for the bombs hitting the Chinese Embassy almost immediately, but that this was not being reported in China. It was also frustrating to see how little was mentioned in the PRC media about the reasons NATO had had for launching its air strikes in the first place. It was very rare before the May 8th Tragedy for Chinese newspapers or television broadcasters to present Milosevic in anything but a positive light.

Then, after the bombs hit the Chinese Embassy, the tendency to present the Serb leader as a hero and "American-led NATO" as responsible for all the troubles that had racked Kosovo grew even more pronounced. The Chinese media also insisted that all explanations of the bombing of the embassy being a "mistake" should be dismissed as Western propaganda. This fed into another, more general, sense of frustration: the inability of Americans to convince most of the Chinese with whom we spoke that it really could have been an admittedly horrendous error.

This kind of frustration was soon matched and sometimes surpassed, however, by a very different sort, which stemmed from my awareness that some Western journalists, pundits, and politicians were saying very misleading things about the Chinese protests. It was galling, for example, to see the protests treated in various op-eds and speeches by American politicians as the result exclusively of government manipulation. Here, students were portrayed as automatons (acting "Borg-like," in the words of a piece in the *Weekly Standard,* a conservative magazine) in the service of a totalitarian state that had allegedly suddenly reverted to using Maoist-style mandatory mass campaigns.

The demonstrations I saw were certainly orchestrated, to a large extent, by the regime. And there definitely were some slogans straight out of the Maoist era ("Down with American Imperialism," for example, had been popular in the 1950s and 1960s). Official youth groups took active roles in the movement, and the police showed, through their non-interference with rock throwers, that the government was willing to look the other way at some violent actions. And so on. Nevertheless, many students chose to take part not because they were told to be outraged but because they genuinely were, and some of them kept calling for a boycott of foreign goods even after the government made it clear that this was not part of the official game plan. Moreover, not all of the slogans were throwbacks to the past; "We are not targets," "Don't talk to us now about human rights," and other new ones were part of the mix. And though the police sanctioned the violence, they also served to limit the extent of it by their very presence and their attempts to control the size of crowds near the Beijing embassies. Beyond all this, at a May 11 Shanghai protest meeting I attended—as the only foreigner, I certainly did feel fear—when the speaker asked the crowd how many of them had taken part in any marches, half raised their hands and half did not. In a totalitarian Borg state, this just does not happen—everyone goes to the march, or at least later pretends to have gone.

Knowing what the mood was in Shanghai, where Americans were rarely sworn at let alone threatened with physical harm during the week following the bombing, the Western media's suggestion that the atmosphere in every city was the same became another source of frustration. The difference between Beijing and Shanghai, where I soon felt very comfortable admitting to being American as opposed to pretending to be Australian—as I had in the capital—was dramatic. In Shanghai, everyone seemed eager to let Americans know that their attitude was different from that of their more politically obsessed Beijing counterparts. Their motto, they told me, was "Zhengfu shi zhengfu, renmin shi renmin" (Governments are governments, people are people), and hence their anger at American leaders should not be construed as anger toward all Americans. For various reasons (its distinctive historical tradition, the unusually large number of people in that city with some kind of ties to Western businesses, and so on), Shanghai was probably exceptional in this regard. I have heard tales by foreigners of what it was like in various other urban centers that suggest my Beijing experiences were more typical than my Shanghai ones. Even days after the public protests stopped, some Americans were still being hassled in various ways in places like Nanjing and Tianjin. Still, the lack of attention to regional variation, due in part to most reporters and camera crews being based in Beijing (and being constrained from traveling easily from place to place due to cumbersome bureaucratic procedures that required them to seek permission to do so ahead of time) was unfortunate. Discussion of local differences would have made clear that the movement was not a homogeneous one—again defying any notion that Chinese youths of 1999 were part of a Borg-like generation.

Relief

One source of relief in Shanghai was that old friends and new acquaintances alike did not seem to feel that it was dangerous to fraternize with an American and be seen doing so. There is always a

danger, when anti-foreign movements break out, that the final targets will not be foreigners at all but those Chinese thought of as having close ties with them or those imagined to have grown too fond of Western ideas. The fact that old friends did not seem ashamed to be seen with me and that people on the street were happy to strike up conversations with me about NATO or about how Shanghai had changed since I lived there in the 1980s was thus a great relief. I can understand why some Western pundits might have thought about the Boxers and the Red Guards of the 1960s when the protests began, since both groups had singled out foreign legations as objects for their rage and had been infuriated by perceived slights to China's national dignity. Still, the vast majority of victims of these two earlier movements were Chinese criticized for being too fond of Western ways—North China Christians, in the one case, alleged "capitalist roaders" in the other. This, if nothing else (and there are many other things) would be enough to make the 1999 protests radically different from events associated with the Boxers and the Red Guards.

There was certainly some concern that the 1999 movement would end up having an adverse impact on the Chinese who worked for American businesses—this may explain why, in fact, I was forbidden from photographing employees inside KFC franchises (though fast food chains are picky about picture-taking even in more ordinary times). There were also some arrests of dissidents, who were accused of having shown, by criticizing the anti-American movement or trying to combine calls for peace in the Balkans with calls for political change within China, that they were "unpatriotic" traitors. There were even reports, though again Shanghai seems to have been the exception as I did not hear about anything of this sort happening there, that some Chinese had been cursed for trying to defend NATO or protect foreigners. Ironically, one group that came under attack in this way was the police, as I have heard that, after May 10, some law enforcement agents in Beijing were taunted for trying to prevent ordinary Chinese from entering the legation area but letting foreigners in. Some frustrated members of the crowd apparently yelled: "What's wrong, don't you like Chinese people? Do you only like foreigners?" Still, there was, overall, very little of this sort of "collateral damage" from the protests—to use that then-fashionable phrase—and this is a source of considerable relief for anyone who knows much about Chinese history.

The banning of American films in the immediate wake of the May 8th Tragedy was a source of disappointment while I was in China but on reflection has become a source of relief. The disappointment stemmed from the fact that I was very bored by the 1950s films celebrating the patriotic efforts of PRC troops in Korea that were substituted for the Hollywood productions originally scheduled to be shown on Chinese television the week I was in Shanghai. The relief came from learning later that one of the films that was supposed to be released in Chinese cities was the Will Smith star-vehicle *Enemy of the State,* which I had watched on the airplane en route to Beijing.

The film presents a very paranoid vision of the technological sophistication and capacity for evil of some within the American government. My first reaction was to hope that my Chinese friends never saw it, as seeing it would only confirm all the worst things about the United States that the PRC official media had been saying in recent years. I was relieved, therefore, that the Chinese government was foolish enough to shoot itself in the foot by keeping people from seeing it. A smarter propaganda organization would have encouraged the citizenry to attend, much as Serbian television had shown a great fondness in 1999 for running *Wag the Dog.*

A final ironic source of relief that came out of initial disappointment: upon arriving in China, I jumped to the conclusion that the educated youths of 1999 were part of a thoroughly apathetic generation, one that was uninterested in pursuing the kinds of bold political initiatives that had seemed to have the potential to do so much good a decade or so earlier, before the brutal crackdown of 1989. One reason for this assumption was that, when I first went to the Internet Café near Beijing University, hoping to see eager young people surfing the web in search of new ideas and information about the outside world, I saw instead the familiar sight of young men playing first person shooter video games. This was not, as I quickly discovered after going on line myself, because all of the good websites were blocked by the government, as only a handful of the many I tried were inaccessible.

I was relieved to discover, as the movement progressed, that the lack of interest in cruising the web that I had witnessed earlier that May did not signify a complete disinterest in politics. Once the protests began, many of the students I encountered became wrapped up in trying to sort out what the events meant and what they could do to make a difference. Admittedly, protesting NATO, which their government was busy criticizing, was a far cry from taking to the streets to demand an end to official corruption, as the students of 1989 had done. Nevertheless, many were clearly getting a kick simply from being able to air opinions and create posters to put on walls, some of which introduced themes that went beyond or veered off from as well as reinforced those trumpeted in the official media. There was a great deal of naiveté to some posters, but there was that too in 1989. There was also this time a great deal of nastiness— "U.S.A." stands for Ugly Shameless Assholes was a Beijing University favorite. But then some of the students who later went to Tiananmen Square in 1989 had taken part in very crude anti-African riots in Nanjing late in 1988, during which crude epithets had been hurled at a foreign group. All this is not to suggest that the students of 1999 were just like those of the 1980s, as they were different in many ways—in part because, since 1989, the government had become a less invasive force in the private lives of young people. It was still a relief of sorts to see, even if the movement they were swept up in had its unsavory side, that a passion for politics was not completely gone from China's campuses.

It is true that the Chinese government succeeded in "riding the tiger" of nationalist outrage in 1999, without coming in for much direct criticism—and managed to do the same thing in the spring of 2005 when issues such as talk of giving Japan a permanent seat on an expanded UN Security Council brought students to the streets. But I am still not convinced this will always be the case. The million dollar question remains whether students inspired by one set of grievances and ideals will ever hook up effectively with workers with differing, though overlapping, sources of anger and reservoirs of hope. Fear of this sort of Solidarity-like phenomenon led the

Two of the most aesthetically appealing posters that students at Fudan University made during the anti-NATO protests. While many youths in Shanghai, as in other cities, simply wrote out angry slogans about "blood debts" needing to be "repaid in blood" or covered their posters with images denigrating Clinton or America, others took the protests as an opportunity to create more imaginative works, or to display their artistic skills. The poster on the left refers to China being transformed by global economic flows; the one on the right publicizes an upcoming protest rally; both make use of vibrant colors. *Photograph by the author.*

government to carry out the massacres of 1989. It was also something that the regime was worried about again in 1999 and also 2005, which helps explain why efforts were soon made in each case to get the students off the streets.

Amusement

It may seem strange to end a piece on a potentially very serious moment in Chinese political life and the history of PRC-American affairs with comments about what I found funny during the week following the May 8th Tragedy and what made my Chinese friends laugh. It was, after all, a period with very somber moments. There was no room for laughter when images of the father of one of the Chinese victims weeping over the body of his daughter were shown on television. There was also no space for levity when news came that the American ambassador was trapped in the Beijing embassy, or when I heard about foreign journalists who had been threatened and Western employees of foreign companies who had had their car windows smashed. There were, nevertheless, many times that week that I laughed and that the Chinese I was around laughed as well, sometimes out of nervousness, admittedly, but often simply out of a sense that funny or absurd things had been said or done.

Ending this chapter with an account of jokes and light moments also seems perfectly in keeping with one of the things that the Shanghai student who told me about the May 11 meeting said when she handed me the set of photos of wall posters. Mixed in with shots of the posters was a photo that surprised me, since it just showed a few friends sitting at a table at a party smiling into the camera. "What is this one doing here," I asked, thinking she had accidentally included a private photo. She responded that she thought it was important for me to have a copy of it as well as the one of wall posters that said things like "Fuck Clinton." The reason was that one of the smiling faces in the picture belonged to a guy who, she said, had been among those yelling anti-American slogans the loudest outside the U.S. consulate in Shanghai on May 9. He was one of the most passionate supporters of the movement, she pointed out, but he had still made it to the birthday party that he had long been planning to attend that night. I should know this, she said, because it demonstrated a key thing about the attitude of Shanghai people, though perhaps not those living in some other parts of China. This was that "Zhengzhi shi zhengzhi, shenghuo shi shenghuo" (Politics is politics, but life is life).

In that spirit, what was funny about that week of rage and frustration? The Li Peng jokes, for starters, though none of these translate well into English and make sense to Americans, so I will skip over them—even the one about the three Chinese leaders and the IQ machine. Also hard to translate, but worth at least trying to, is one that apparently made the rounds at Beijing's Qinghua campus on May 9. This had to do with a group of students who had been making preparations to head down to the American Embassy to throw rocks, but had decided that since rocks were heavy and hard to find, they would settle for taking tomatoes. Then, however, one member of the group got hungry and by the time they got to the embassy, he had eaten up all the ammo, so they were back to square one, all revved up but nothing to throw.

There were also inadvertent sources of humor. For example, across the street from one of the busiest Shanghai branches of McDonald's, some protesters put up a four-character sign, one word per piece of paper, that can be translated as "Don't Buy American Goods." I saw this on May 10 but by the following day, the first two pieces of paper had fallen off, so all that was left was "American Goods." What made this especially funny is that the character for "America" can also mean "beautiful," so the net effect was an inadvertent coup for McDonald's—a free advertisement telling passersby that lovely things could be bought across the street.

Another source of amusement associated with fast food came when I passed a store selling banners and saw one in the window for KFC. Remembering my colleague working on the symbolism of the Colonel, I went in to see if I could buy it, or rather the Chinese friend I was with asked if I could. Assuming that I couldn't speak Chinese, the people in the store said that because I was from that imperialist land of America, it probably wouldn't hurt to let me buy it, but they wouldn't want my friend to buy it for herself, as that would be unpatriotic. When I broke in, in Chinese, saying that all this imperialist really cared about was how much the banner cost, they found this terribly funny (and, after some good-natured haggling, let me have it quite cheap).

Something else I said that week, which wasn't initially intended as a joke but I started to tell as one after I realized that it made some people laugh and could break the tension when I was in groups where I was the only Westerner, had to do with the Vietnam War. In Shanghai, after going through a kind of ritualized conversation that began with me admitting to being American, and then the person I was speaking to saying they did not hate me, just my government, I often mentioned my own experience with anti-war movements. "I used to march against American imperialism in my youth," I would say, and almost inevitably, the other person would find this very funny. (There were, of course, many differences between what the students were doing on the streets of China in 1999 and the events I took part in as a kid growing up in Los Angeles in the late 1960s and early 1970s. The government was not supportive of the anti-war rallies of my childhood, for example. And the demonstrations I went to with my parents always had better music. I believed in the cause, as best as I could understand it at the age of 9 or 10, but I was eager to go in large part because someone like Joan Baez might show up.)

Even though there were many differences between the two contexts, I did not draw analogies with anti–Vietnam War rallies purely as a lark. I thought it important, among other things, to underscore to the Chinese I met that Americans do not always support everything their government does. There were also some things that did remind me of the 1960s and early 1970s about the things I was seeing on China's streets and reading in its newspapers. The peace dove was almost as common a part of wall posters as the target symbol, and at Beijing University there was a call for "peace and music" that was reminiscent of the "make love not war" chants I remember. Even the use of profanity was not so different, as I can recall the emotional charge of shouting out "One, Two, Three, Four, We Don't Want Your Fucking War" as a kid.

I was also struck by the Vietnam War–era feel of an ad that ran in Beijing's official English-language Chinese newspaper, *China Daily*, which showed a multicultural group of children with a target symbol superimposed over them. Admittedly, the target symbol and Benetton-ad type of photo was pure 1990s, but the words that accompanied it were "Give Peace a Chance."*

Another source of amusement came from the response I got to one of my efforts to defuse tension in conversations with Chinese friends whenever the issue of fear came up. When asked in Shanghai if I had been scared in Beijing on the night of May 9—which people sometimes did in part to make sure I grasped how much more civilized their city was when it came to protests these days—I developed a stock response. I was not afraid of this sort of anti-imperialist movement, which seemed in part a holdover of old ideas and patterns, I would say. What scared me more were some of the new phenomena I saw around me in China, from the extent of environmental degradation, to the growing number of homeless on the streets, to the things I heard about working conditions in some factories and rising unemployment rates. Drawing attention to these sorts of problems is no joke, of course, but I would get a laugh nonetheless when I summed up my feelings by saying that I tended to find the lingering hold of nationalistic Chinese communism less scary than the birth pangs of Chinese capitalism. The notion that a visitor from the most powerful capitalist country on earth would be more afraid of capitalism than Communism was always good for a laugh—though, to me, it remains very black humor indeed.

Two Postscripts: One about Humility, One about Arnold

After returning from China in 1999, I began to associate the anti-NATO protests with yet another feeling: humility. This is because of a humbling experience I had when, at Indiana University, I proudly showed a bright student in one of my classes, who expressed interest in hearing more about my adventures in China in 1999, a favorite, though blurry, photograph I had taken. Shot in Beijing during an anti-NATO demonstration, what excited me about the photograph

---

* This led me to quip, predictably, that the language of Lennon as well as that of Lenin seemed to shape political discourse in late twentieth-century China—a weak attempt at humor that was completely lost on the Chinese friend to whom I made it.

was the shirt that one of the protesters was wearing, which had on it a globally familiar image of Che Guevara. My gloss on this photograph, which Americans of my own age and older to whom I had previously shown it had readily accepted, was that it captured something very fitting, even amusing. Here was my take on the picture: in going to what was essentially a Yankee Go Home march with Chinese characteristics, the young man in the picture had put on a shirt emblazoned with the face of an activist who was associated with criticism of American imperialism during an earlier era.

The American student I showed the photograph to, however, just shook his head when I gave this explanation. "You just don't get it," he said, "do you?" When I asked him to explain, he continued: "Look what the guy next to him is wearing: a Kurt Cobain shirt." He proceeded to tell me that this suggested different readings of the two shirts, especially since the Che image I had found so interesting was probably best known to the wearer because it had been used on the cover of a recording by Rage Against the Machine, an American rock group. The wearers of the two shirts were probably friends who had just decided to don favorite pieces of clothing—each associated with people who had died young, each associated with rock groups, as Cobain had been lead singer of Nirvana—to wear to the march. Che and Rage Against the Machine and Kurt Cobain and Nirvana all had links to youthful rebellion, he admitted, but the Yankee Go Home twist seemed quite a stretch to him. And I have to admit, he is probably right.

Finally I want to mention, in case Schwarzenegger ends up reading this in print (especially if he is still governor of the state that employs me when he does so), that I never did really think Arnold was a wimp to back out of that China trip. He may well have cancelled his 1999 trip at the behest of his Chinese hosts. And, if he *was* just a little bit scared, it was probably because he made the natural mistake of failing to take some of the things being said about China at the time with the grain of salt they deserved. If you just read the China bashers, who in May of 1999 were in a triumphal mood, it would have been all too easy—though wrong—to have accepted then the idea that China was a scarily Borg-like land of conformity that never changed.

Perhaps, though, Arnold's move from films to politics has made him a more skeptical reader of "China Threat" media, less ready to accept that Borg-like populations are to be found in the real world and not just in sci-fi scripts. After all, he went to the PRC late in 2005 to promote increased economic activity between that country and California, just a few months after the *Atlantic Monthly* came out with a lead story suggesting that a U.S. war with China could easily break out soon.

10. Karl Gets a New Cap: Budapest in 2000

"Do you need a McDonald's," my Hungarian colleague Maria asked, "or should we head straight out to Statue Park?" References to the Golden Arches had become a code word between us from the moment I had wondered, earlier in the day, what she thought of the appearance of local fast food chains and other signs of Americanization scattered throughout the city. She had pondered this for a moment, then replied pragmatically that she didn't like Big Macs or fries, but she certainly appreciated the fact that the toilets were always clean wherever they were sold. "I'm fine," I said, a bit impatiently, in response to her question, "let's head straight to the park." I added that seeing Szoborpark was my "main reason for coming to Budapest this time."

I actually had other reasons as well for returning to the city, which I had first visited in the spring of 1999 to attend a conference held at Central European University. The day before the one we had set aside for sightseeing, for example, I had given a talk on human rights and the Chinese Revolution at CEU, and I had also delivered some Chinese political posters and other materials to the Open Society Archive, an affiliated institution, for use in a pair of upcoming exhibits they were planning.

Still, my statement had a kernel of truth to it. I had heard about Statue Park during my last stay but had not been able fit a visit into my schedule and had determined that seeing it would be a top priority if I ever returned. The notion of visiting this final resting place for "GIGANTIC MEMORIALS FROM THE COMMUNIST DICTATORSHIP" (how a tourist map describes it) appealed to me a great deal from the start. And I was intrigued by the fact that, while statues from the Soviet era had been destroyed or sold to collectors in most other parts of central and eastern Europe, they had been theme-parked in Hungary. Surely, I thought, there was an important message here about intra-regional differences—differences that, growing up in America during the Cold War with only a casual interest in Soviet Bloc countries, I had hardly thought about or even realized existed.

The colleague who had offered to take me around town during my return visit to Budapest knew of my eagerness to get the "glance behind the Iron Curtain" offered by Statue Park (as the tourist map also put it). Maria insisted, though, that our first stop would not be there but rather the Parliament building, a beautifully appointed nineteenth-century edifice. Her idea was that we should do so simply to see when tours were available later in the day, buy a ticket for one of these, and then return at a pre-arranged time. When it turned out that a tour would be starting soon, however, and tickets for it were still available, the only sensible thing to do seemed to be to visit that building first—hence my impatience when she asked me if I needed a McDonald's.

The Parliament was, I have to admit, if a bit grudgingly, a very interesting building to see, filled with its own share of monuments from bygone times and not as similar as I had worried it might be to comparable grand edifices I had seen in western European cities. And, to be fair, I should admit as well that the visit was especially illuminating due to the company I was in: my personal escort, an economist who has done very interesting work comparing Hungary and China, kept up a sotto voce commentary

in one of my ears that contradicted many things the official
guide said.

The general thing that annoyed Maria most was the guide's con-
tinual effort to give the impression that the country's pre-
Communist and post-Communist eras were seamlessly linked. This,
my companion insisted, was done to create a misleading sense of
continuity that fits in with efforts to celebrate the notion that 2000
had a doubly millennial meaning in Hungary, marking the passage
of two thousand years of Christianity and one thousand years of enduring Hungarian nationhood.

Especially troubling to my friend was the late 1990s relocation of
the Crown Jewels of Hungary's former ruling family, which had just
been moved to a display case built at the very center of the Parliament building, where they were continually guarded by a pair of
Buckingham Palace–type soldiers. (That we happened to get to see
the changing of the guard was a small pleasure for me. On the other
hand, it was just a further source of annoyance for my companion,
especially when she got chided by an officious employee of the museum security staff for wandering too close to the jewels and the
guards.)

The official guide insisted that the decision to move the old Hungarian crown, complete with its curious bent cross, and other icons
of monarchy back to the Parliament was done by virtue of popular
demand. The people wanted them there, she claimed, just as she
had claimed that the people were enthusiastic about the double-
millennium's arrival.

My escort would have none of this. The placement of the Crown
Jewels was just an effort by the current government, she countered,
to play the nationalism card in a way that would help buttress its position and undermine that of its opponents. Cynical manipulations
of symbols and vacuous references to public opinion, she suggested,
were trademarks of the then-current government, an odd coalition
of members of right-wing groups and members of a formerly progressive and now seemingly just opportunistic party known as the
Young Democrats.

Apparently—and here I am piecing together things told me by various people—this coalition had been trying to define contemporary

politics in such a way that anything linked to the pre-Communist era would appear good, anything from the Communist era or even tangentially linked to it bad. Now, so many people suffered in so many ways during the decades preceding the late 1980s that at least the second half of this equation may seem unproblematic or at least harmless. It had, however, some disturbing implications. Not only were all former Communist Party members discredited in this political vision, but so too were many others—including, ironically, some of the leading anti-Communist dissidents of the 1970s and 1980s. This was because, the coalition had implied or stated, by helping to orchestrate the famous "handshake transition" of 1988 and 1989, once held up as a model process of moving away from Communism, these dissidents had been far too conciliatory toward those on the opposite side of the fence. The ability to help develop a strategy to change regimes without bloodshed and a minimum of vilification, it now seemed, was supposed to be seen as a flaw, not a virtue. This was the charge leveled at the New Democrats, the erstwhile allies, but by the year 2000, opponents of the Young Democrats—the leaders of which were too young in the late 1980s to play central roles in the transition.

Through this kind of rhetoric, the New Democrats, some of whose members played pivotal roles not just in bringing about the fall of communism but also in laying the ideological groundwork for that fall, were being left out in the cold. The Young Democrats, meanwhile, had found a justification, in this all-or-nothing form of retrospective and pure anti-communism, for allying themselves with rightwing groups. They did this even if it meant working closely with organizations whose members embraced a form of virulent nationalism that had a strong racial and ethnic component. They did it even if it placed them in the curious position of being a party that had the words "young" and "democrats" in its name, yet embraced old monarchical symbols.

Finally, and most troubling and ironic of all, the move toward linking the pre-Communist and post-Communist eras had been accompanied by a worrisome return of some features of the Communist period itself. The press was increasingly being brought under state control, for example, I was told. In addition, there had been an escalation of a Manichean style of rhetoric. One had to be either a friend or an enemy of the nation, just as one formerly was considered to be either a friend or enemy of the Party. Some features of the Communist era remained dead and buried, of course, and signs of economic openness and cosmopolitan cultural life were still everywhere in Budapest those days. And yet, echoes of the recent past disguised as a nationalist hymn to the merging of pre-Communist traditions and post-Communist rebirth could make for unpleasant listening for some people—my friend and sometime fellow sightseer very much included.

As much as I ended up enjoying our tour of the Parliament, and as grateful as I was for all I learned from the contrasting accounts of its political meaning I heard as we looked at the building's often stunning nineteenth-century decorations, I was itching to get to Statue Park by the time the McDonald's issue came up. Even after settling that and taking the tram to Maria's car, though, it still took some time to reach this elusive destination. Szoborpark, it seems, is just not very easy to find—even for someone such as Maria who lives in Budapest. It was created so that local people—as well as tourists—would be reminded of and educated about the Communist era. But due either to the price of land in the city proper or a desire to allow those who wished to forget to have an easier time doing that, the "most exciting outdoor museum in Eastern Europe" (the tourist map again) was placed outside of town. Moreover, there were not many signs telling drivers how exactly to get there.

In any case, if they were there, we did not see them, and as a result ended up getting lost. This added a couple of new items to our itinerary that neither my companion nor I had in mind when we set out. One was a brief stop in a parking lot that, fittingly enough, was that of a roadside McDonald's. From here, my escort called her husband on her mobile phone to see if he could explain where she had made a wrong turn, receiving instructions to detour through a nearby town. This town, she told me as we headed there, had an interesting history. It had originally been occupied by immigrants from Germany and was a place where German was the main language spoken. In the aftermath of World War II, most of its occupants were deported to Germany, making it a ghost town of sorts.

Now, however, some of the earlier residents or their descendants were migrating back into the community, and a mixture of Hungarian and German could be heard spoken on the streets and in the shops.

On our way into this town, whose German *and* Hungarian names I immediately forgot in an egalitarian fashion, we had to pass along a small road that had, by its side, a giant junkyard filled with old red telephone booths.* "I guess this is our day for seeing ghosts and cemeteries," was my friend's only comment about this surreal roadside sight.

When we finally arrived at the Statue Park, I was afraid I might be disappointed, having built it up so much in my mind. I wasn't. The statues were fascinating to look at, both in terms of form and the descriptions of what they represented. They were, I was pleased to discover, much more varied in style than I had expected. They were also more animated than I expected, with some figures looking as though they were about to leap or in one case even fly off their pedestals. There was even a statue of a sculptor working on creating a monument, a precociously postmodern touch in a park filled with icons of high modernism.

The grounds were, moreover, laid out in an interesting manner, so that one could stroll among the statues in a pleasant way. The whole effect was not unlike that of a Roman ruin, with the statues of faceless workers and famous theorists and political leaders taking the place of the isolated columns of a second-century AD building. In both cases, the effect is to remind the visitor that a once proud civilization was here but now has crumbled.

One added twist, though, that has no Roman ruin counterpart, was the soundtrack. When you enter Statue Park, there are revolutionary songs playing and, as you look at the monuments, you can sometimes hear their strains in the background. Thinking about the music, I realized again what lucky company I was in, as my companion could and did sing along with many of the anthems. She

---

* In preparing this manuscript, I asked my 2000 guide to remind me of the names of the town: just for the record, they are Budaörs (in Hungarian) and Wudersch (in German).

One of the transplanted monuments at Statue Park outside Budapest. *Photograph by Ivan Soros, used by permission.*

told me, from time to time during our visit, of some of the ways that friends and members of her family had suffered during the Communist period. But this did not prevent her from continuing to find some of the songs inspiring or simply pleasing in a nostalgic sort of way, something that is true as well with some of my Chinese friends and music associated with the Cultural Revolution.

I was enjoying my visit so much, at first, that I found myself wondering what another Hungarian colleague, whose opinions on historical and political issues I respect a great deal, had meant by a comment he had made the previous day. The idea of having such a park is wonderful, he had said, but there is a serious flaw to it. He would not explain what he meant when I pressed him, saying it was better for me to just see what I made of the place.

About half-way through my tour of the park, perhaps in part because of what I had seen and heard at the Parliament building, the penny dropped and I knew what he meant. Or, rather, something hit me that may have been what my friend with the misgivings had had in mind when he made the comment. Whether or not it was, the phenomenon, once noticed, was disturbing.

My awareness of it came while I was scrutinizing a monument commemorating the valor of Hungarian socialists who had gone off to Spain to fight Franco in the 1930s. One problem with Statue Park, I realized, is that it flattens out history. This was, in a sense, the same thing that my escort had insisted was wrong with the official guide's presentation of the Parliament. The difference is that in that setting it was links between the pre-Communist era and the present that were made to appear too seamless. Here, the way the statues were arrayed went too far in making the Communist period and indeed everything in any way associated with Marxism and Leninism seem isolated from all other aspects of history.

Surely, even if one has no love of Communist Party rule in any form, it is worth maintaining a distinction between those who went off to fight fascism in the 1930s and those who joined state-sponsored militias inside Hungary that were used to suppress the 1956 Revolution. And yet, the monuments to those who took part in the two crusades—one to oppose and the other to protect a form of authoritarian rule—are displayed in the park as though the participants were doing the same type of thing, inspired by the same ideas. What exactly is the message, then, that schoolchildren are supposed to take away from the park? It is certainly good to preserve elements of the past, but arranging them to flatten out a varied history has a troubling side. Leaving objects largely open to interpretation, as the park does, is also a valuable thing to do—in some contexts. I left wondering, though, if given what I had heard at the Parliament building and learned in other conversations with Hungarians who were critical of authoritarianism, past and present, right or left in orientation, whether Budapest just now is one of those contexts.

Troubled by those thoughts, I was pleased when Maria told me a little story about the kind of use of old monuments that she thought was best of all. Students at a local economics institute lobbied after 1989 to have one of the old statues from their campus left in place. Lenin could go, they said, but why not leave Marx in place? He was, after all, a great nineteenth-century economist. And after the statue was left in place, it started being put to new uses, integrated back into the life of the community in novel ways. Most notably, on St. Nicholas Day, a red cap would be put on Marx's head, transforming him from a precursor of Lenin and Stalin to a Santa Claus figure of sorts. And, around examination time, students would implore this hybrid patron saint of change or of good luck or of who knows what to help them do well on their tests.

I am not quite sure what my friend's story means and whether it has a moral. I do know, though, that if I make a third visit to Budapest, it will probably be in December. There is one more statue I need to see.

11. Patriotism in Public Life: The United States in 2001

I hate the first person plural . . . I grew up with "we" and "us" . . . listening to speeches saying, "Comrades, we must . . ." . . . I experienced the same phenomenon in journalism . . . the journalism of endless editorials, in which "we" explained to "us" what "we" all needed to understand.
    —Slavenka Drakulić, *Café Europa: Life After Communism,* 1996

To a degree, such deference [by newscasters in the weeks following September 11] reflects TV's customary rallying around the flag in time of national crisis. Such a stance is understandable; in light of the enormity of the [September 11] attacks, even atheists are singing "God Bless America." But . . . the repeated references to "we" and "us" . . . have violated every canon of good journalism.
    —Michael Massing, *The Nation,* October 15, 2001

Like many Americans who study China, I experience a pleasant culture shock whenever I return from the PRC. This comes from being reminded afresh of just how different the U.S. and China are when it comes to everything from the amount of public space given over to celebrating the political status quo to the diversity of print and broadcast media. When I have just returned, it feels better than ever to pick up a newspaper (knowing there will be editorial cartoons like *Doonesbury* that mock government officials) and even to channel surf (knowing that I can choose from many stations that will air different sorts of shows). It is also exciting to rejoin the academic life of a campus where students are encouraged to critically assess everything (even the things I tell them in lectures) and avoid group-think approaches to issues. Reading *Café Europa* (a work by an Eastern European author whose earlier collection of essays, *How We Survived Communism—and Even Laughed,* I had taught to good effect in a class on women and revolution) helped me clarify what returning from the PRC has always meant for me. Re-entering makes me appreciate anew how stifling it can be to spend time in a place—even one you love—where life is lived largely in the first-person plural.

Perhaps it is because I so value this feeling upon return that it disturbed me to discover, in the months immediately following 9/11, how often I was having flashbacks to time spent in the PRC. This happened when I heard commentators extol "patriotic education," a term I had previously associated with China's Communist Party. It happened when I saw political messages (such as "United We Stand") appear in display spaces normally reserved for ads for products. It happened when I read that a White House spokesman had told Americans to "watch what they say"—and then again when I read that, in an official transcript of his statement, the phrase "watch what they say," in Orwellian fashion, had disappeared. Colleagues who grew up in or used to regularly visit Soviet bloc countries also described experiencing the same sort of disquieting flashback moments during the final months of 2001—and the flashbacks, though less common now than at first, have continued to take place from time to time, whenever the rhetoric of the "War on Terror" is taken to a new height by the president or exaggerated claims about how "effectively" the United States has pursued its goals in Iraq are made by the administration.

When patriotic symbols were suddenly everywhere late in 2001 and pundits began insisting that the terrorists had "underestimated" American power and resolve, I was reminded most directly of all of the time I spent in the PRC two-and-a-half years previously.

Many Chinese were convinced in 1999 that the U.S. government had tried to blow up their embassy in Belgrade, and a common cry was that America would eventually regret its failure to appreciate just how strong China and its people were. And no matter which TV station I turned to in Beijing and Shanghai that May, I saw images of destruction and heard newscasters using the first-person plural.

On reflection, I knew late in 2001 that there were many differences between what was occurring here in the wake of September 11 and what went on in the PRC in the wake of the embassy bombing. In a truly Orwellian state, after all, the press would not have been able to note the changes from speech to transcript described above. Nor would Susan Sontag's provocative piece in the September 24, 2001, issue of the *New Yorker* have been able to appear. She got an enormous amount of flack for referring there to Bush as a "robotic" president and insisting that suicide hijackers might be many things but certainly not cowards. She was not, however, arrested. Nor did the FBI jam all websites that carried her essay or try to halt sales of that edition of the *New Yorker.* So people were free to go to newsstands or libraries or cruise the web and make up their own minds about Sontag's claims that television coverage of 9/11 had been "infantalizing" and that quickly called, near unanimous votes should always worry democratic citizens.

In addition, I knew in those tense months that, even in such a time of crisis, there would still be some space made available within the U.S. on campuses and elsewhere (though perhaps not enough) for wide-ranging discussion of official policies. There was also some room for ongoing public debate over who should get to define love of country. In contrast, the price in the PRC for contesting the official version of patriotism has often been death, as was demonstrated in the 1989 massacre, which crushed a movement carried out in the name of *jiuguo* or "saving the nation"—from corruption above all else.

Still, though I knew about all those differences, I remained disconcerted in the final months of 2001 by those PRC flashbacks, since I wanted to be able, once again, to take for granted that there was a chasm, not merely a gap, between the public sphere here and the public sphere there. The ability to live outside of an oppressive "we" began to seem to me a fragile thing indeed. And perhaps, even in the freest societies, I found myself thinking, the collapse of a vibrant public sphere worthy of the name was always just a few crises away from dissolution.

One thing I should make clear is that I never thought, as some Chinese claimed on electronic bulletin boards and in interviews with foreign journalists, that the horrors of September 11 were analogous to the Belgrade embassy bombing or "May 8th Tragedy." The difference in scale alone undermined this notion: three killed in one case, thousands in the other. In addition, I continued to think in 2001 that May 8 was probably the result of a very stupid and regrettable blunder—of the sort that not long before had led NATO planes to crash into an Italian ski lift. There is no question that September 11 was the result of meticulous planning. My point, then, is not that I ever saw May 8 and September 11 as comparable—just that the aftermath of each felt too similar for my comfort. For example:

There was a fascination in each instance with analogies to mid-twentieth-century battles. Comments about September 11 as Pearl Harbor revisited saturated the media here; Chinese television stations ran old Korean War films in 1999.

In China in 1999, as in the U.S. late in 2001, many newspaper headlines described specific foreign political leaders expressing their solidarity with a country in mourning. This was done to show that a rise of patriotism had international support.

Last of all is the obvious parallel: the lashing out that occurred against people who looked a certain way. I witnessed some of this firsthand in Beijing on May 9, when I ventured into that city's consular district. I was not terribly scared, since police were present to ensure that things did not get out of hand. And I was not alone but rather part of a group of Westerners, one of whom had suggested that we all familiarize ourselves with the Chinese for "I am from Australia"—just in case. None of us were physically assaulted. Nevertheless, it was disturbing to have several people look at me and spit and to have one man, after asking if I was American, tell me (before I could answer) that if I was he would like to kill me. I remembered how I felt then whenever I read in 2001 of an Arab-American being taunted or struck.

It is true that many people in the U.S. were deeply concerned late in 2001 about September 11 triggering a xenophobic backlash; that campus officials issued statements telling students not to discriminate against their peers from foreign countries; that President George W. Bush quickly called on Americans not to view all Muslims as terrorists; and that not all parts of the U.S. were equally rife with prejudice. Yet similar points could be made about China in 1999. The Communist Party tried to steer the protests, but it also made efforts to protect foreign lives, and campus officials did their part to try to keep students from acting in xenophobic ways. As for local variation, as noted in a couple of earlier chapters, when I traveled to Shanghai on May 10 I found the mood there (on campuses and elsewhere) much less charged with hostility directed at individual foreigners than had been the case in Beijing. Once I got there, I stopped worrying about whether I should pretend to be Australian. And within days of the embassy bombing, high-ranking PRC ministers announced that, while China's people should make known their anger at NATO, harming foreign visitors was wrong.

I know that in times of uncertainty people reach for analogies to make sense of and assert some control over troubling situations. And I know that these analogies can easily become overdrawn, stretched too far. 9/11 was not just like Pearl Harbor nor like anything else. And the reaction to it was not just like the reaction in China to May 8.

What disturbed me late in 2001 was simply that I had to remind myself of ways that being in the PRC was different from being in the United States. What I longed for was to be able to feel the difference again without thinking. President Bush and others spoke of the need for Americans to regain a sense of normalcy. For me, I guess, part of what I needed to do to regain that feeling was to be able to stop having to remind myself how much freedom I enjoyed. Sometimes during the years that have followed, I have been able to stop reminding myself of the contrasts. From time to time, though, the flashbacks come again. There is a big difference between a president who claims that his administration has the right to carry out wiretaps without going to a court first to get permission and a Chinese leadership that makes far greater and more regular transgressions against the personal freedoms of those it governs. Sometimes, though, the difference still just doesn't feel like the kind of night and day one that it once did.

12. A San Francisco of the East:
Hong Kong in 2002

Soon after it became a Crown Colony of the British in 1842, Hong Kong began to seem to visitors and be presented to readers as a wondrous place, as two nineteenth-century texts mentioned previously illustrate. Here, for example, is how Jules Verne, whose knowledge of the Crown Colony was drawn exclusively from armchair excursions there of various sorts, describes the city in *Around the World in Eighty Days:* "Docks, hospitals, wharves, a Gothic cathedral, a government house, macadamised streets, give to Hong Kong the appearance of a town in Kent or Surrey transferred by some strange magic to the antipodes." And here is how, in *A Journey to the East,* Li Gui, the real-life Chinese counterpart to the Jules Verne–creation Phileas Fogg, describes the city he visited near the end of his actual—as opposed to imaginary—round-the-world trip: "On the sea, the merchant ships are many, their masts standing up like chopsticks. . . . [At night] lamps illuminate everything brilliantly with countless thousands of lights—a magnificent spectacle."

Coming to Hong Kong early in 1987, after almost six months of living in Shanghai (before it began to undergo the post-1990 re-internationalization that has been alluded to throughout this book), I found wondrous some of the same things that Verne and Li draw attention to in their works, despite all of the changes that had taken place in the city during the century or so that had passed. I was excited by parts of Hong Kong that seemed as though they had been "transferred by some magic" to the other side of the world—though, in my case, what excited me was less the sight of Western-style buildings (Shanghai had those lining its famous Bund) than the sight of menus featuring every kind of European cuisine and movie theaters showing the latest Hollywood films (Shanghai had both of these things in the 1930s and has them again today, but did not have either in the 1980s). And, like Li Gui, I was overwhelmed by the view of the city from the harbor, especially at night—though by 1987, the visual effects were a bit different, including as they did a lot of neon and sets of flashing lights of varied colors that would seem to chase one another around the edges of some of the tallest skyscrapers.

I was primed to find Hong Kong a city of wonders in part because of the looks of envy Anne (my wife) and I got from Shanghainese friends when we told them we would be going there. We would be taking the trip during the long Spring Festival (Chinese New Year). This vacation finally allowed Anne to take a break from her heavy work load as an English teacher, gave me an excuse to take a break from mining local archives (which would be closed for a time due to the holiday anyway) in search of clues about student protest activity between 1919 and 1949, and provided the two of us a chance to see other parts of China. We would go to Kunming, which is near Burma in beautiful Yunnan province first, then Guilin, which is famed for its mountains that seem to rise from nowhere, and then head to Canton and from there to the nearby Crown Colony.

I told our friends that I had some research to do in Hong Kong, and would be giving a talk at a university on what I had found so far in my archival digging. It was clear, though, that in their minds, Hong Kong was not associated with the work and study I would be doing there. It was, rather, a fantasyland of excitement and consumption, a setting where goods from every corner of the earth could be bought. They clearly expected us to spend more time sightseeing, eating out, seeing films, and shopping than searching for documents and meeting scholars, and they wanted to hear all about it when we returned.

My subsequent trips to Hong Kong have all been very different and, though I continue to like the city, I no longer think of it as magical. One thing that is different now is that, if I go there after spending time in Shanghai, my Shanghainese friends do not seem particularly envious or even all that curious about Hong Kong being my next destination. This is partly because Hong Kong is now part of the PRC. But that is not the only reason. After all, back in 1996, when I told my friends in Shanghai that I would soon go from their city to Hong Kong, they did not think it a big deal at all—and that was a year *before* the Crown Colony "returned to the embrace of the ancestral homeland" (as PRC publicity typically describes the transfer of control that took place July 1, 1997). That people in Shanghai were already blasé about Hong Kong at that point was due to the fact that by the mid-1990s their own city had become such an exciting place to spend time. And such a good place to shop, thanks to the arrival of fancy new department stores, many of them bankrolled by Hong Kong investors. Another thing that has changed my feeling about Hong Kong has been the need I feel now to be watchful when I am there for signs of economic and, even more so, cultural decay. In the mid-1990s, with its long period as a British Crown Colony drawing to a close, Western commentators sometimes wrote about Hong Kong's future in dire terms. It was likened in one editorial I remember (and the simile resonated with much general discussion of the time) to a canary about to enter a mine shaft, and we would just need to wait and see if it could survive in its new Communist-run environment. Given that background, it is perhaps not surprising that, on recent visits, I have often gotten an odd feeling, which is a bit like that one might have on running into an old friend who was diagnosed with a terminal disease, yet seems in pretty good shape. One feels relief but also asks uncomfortable questions. Is he really all right—or just putting up a brave front? Was he misdiagnosed—or is he in remission?

The doomsayers prepared us for many dismal things to take place very quickly after the July 1, 1997, Hong Kong handover, an event eagerly anticipated by the Beijing regime, which put up a countdown clock in Tiananmen Square to tick off the seconds until it took place. There would be mass arrests at the annual June 4th rallies of remembrance, held to commemorate the Beijing massacre of 1989, we were warned. Legislative bodies would be disbanded. International investors would stop viewing Hong Kong as a good place to put their money. Land values would plummet. Economic collapse. And so on. None of these things have occurred, yet many foreign China specialists, including myself, remain too unsure about where Hong Kong is heading to declare the patient completely out of danger.

This is because the portents can be so confusing. During a single return visit, I may spend one day marveling about still being able to buy books on and by people like the Dalai Lama that are banned on the mainland, and the next day worrying about the news that an independently minded journalist has been fired. I will meet a local optimist one day, who stresses that her metropolis has defied the naysayers to remain a financial hub, and then encounter a local pessimist who—knowing that Hong Kong's post-1949 development was fueled largely by an influx of people and capital from Shanghai—insists that the rise of Pudong (East Shanghai) will precipitate his city's fall.

When I stopped off in Hong Kong in November of 2002, my tendency to swing between hope and despair during a single visit was especially pronounced. Timing had a lot to do with this. I arrived just as the Sixteenth Congress of the Chinese Communist Party (CCP) began, then took a quick trip to Nanjing mid-way through those meetings, and came back to Hong Kong briefly before heading back to the States.

My optimism about Hong Kong was fueled on that trip by tracking the different ways a major national news story was handled in the former Crown Colony and on the mainland. All Nanjing newspapers carried identical reports and had the same stock words of praise for Jiang Zemin (as he stepped down from leading the Standing Committee of the Politburo) and for his successor Hu Jintao.

The coverage in Hong Kong newspapers, by contrast, was impressively wide-ranging. There was certainly nothing in any mainland publication like the cynical political cartoons that greeted me in *The Apple,* a provocative Hong Kong newspaper, when I returned from Nanjing. One of these, linked to a story about Jiang holding on to the reins of the military, showed the "retiring" leader smiling smugly behind a curtain, while Hu stood in front of it looking uneasy. Another showed Jiang and Hu as two members of a relay team whose members were not quite clear on how the race was supposed to be run, with the former shown pretending to pass but actually clinging to the baton while the latter tried to surge forward.

Grounds for pessimism, meanwhile, were provided by the main local story making headlines that November: the impending implementation of "Article 23" of the Basic Law, the general blueprint worked out in 1990 that provided the contours for how Hong Kong would be run when the Crown Colony became a Special Administrative Region of the PRC. The Basic Law was predicated on the idea that the territory would retain a "high degree of autonomy" for fifty years after 1997, but also included stipulations making it clear that Beijing would play an important role in shaping social and political life in Hong Kong. Article 23 specified that post-handover Hong Kong would enact laws to prevent acts of treason against the PRC from taking place within its borders, but the Basic Law itself did not say exactly what those laws would look like. The 2002 debate was over a set of proposals that the local authorities were considering to bring a kind of "USA Patriot Act" with some special twists into being, which proponents said would simply carry out the mission of the Basic Law, but opponents objected to as going much too far in limiting civil liberties in the name of protecting state security, and being framed too much to serve Beijing's as opposed to Hong Kong's best interests.*

---

* The issue was not whether laws on sedition needed to be drafted—similar statutes, after all, operate in many countries and operated in Hong Kong when it was under British rule—but how broadly treason would be defined and how limited opportunities for open debate on the topic had been up to that point. Thanks in large part to a series of often impressively large protests by local residents who were once thought to be thoroughly "apolitical," the version of Article 23 that was almost implemented in 2002 was tabled, revised, and had still not been passed and put into effect as of early 2007.

Torn between optimism and pessimism about the future, I ended my 2002 visit immersing myself in the local past by spending an afternoon at the city's museum of history. Its main exhibit, "The Hong Kong Story," is made up of an impressive and eclectic set of multimedia displays (films, photographs, and artifacts are all part of the mix, as are wax figures, including ones that show Margaret Thatcher and Deng Xiaoping agreeing on the terms of the handover) that take the visitor from pre-historic times up to 1997. Anyone vexed by coming to terms with contemporary Hong Kong should make a point of visiting it. Seeing it won't turn an optimist into a pessimist or vice versa, but it can certainly help outsiders put current dilemmas into clearer perspective. For example, it will quickly disabuse of their misconceptions any Westerners who arrive with the misguided notion that Hong Kong was idyllic and free before 1997. The museum's main exhibit, which was still essentially unchanged when I saw it a second time in July 2005, notes that before the most powerful local official in Hong Kong had to answer to Beijing, he answered to a more distant capital: London. And that for decades Chinese had to receive special dispensation to buy property in the attractive Victoria Peak district.

Anyone fretting that Hong Kong has become just like any mainland city can, meanwhile, take heart from the fact that the exhibit refers openly to the outpouring of local support for the Tiananmen protesters. Urban centers to the north may be able to compete with Hong Kong now when it comes to freedom of consumption, but they lag far behind when it comes to broaching taboo subjects like this in public settings, just as the former Crown Colony remains the only part of the PRC where June 4th memorial rallies are held each year.

What, though, of economic pessimism? Even here, the exhibit offers some hope by reminding us that Hong Kong has often reinvented itself. (One of the best parts of the exhibit details one such re-invention circa 1960—as an exotic destination for culturally curious tourists.) If Shanghai is luring investors who would have once looked to Hong Kong, this need not signal disaster—just the need for yet another reinvention.

Here, a California analogy comes to mind. Los Angeles was once in San Francisco's economic shadow. When the reverse became true, San Francisco did not cease to be a great city. It just became a different sort of great city. One that made the most of spectacular hills and a beautiful harbor . . . two things that Hong Kong most definitely has.

PART FOUR

THE TOMORROWLAND DIARIES

One of the many bookstores on Shanghai's Fuzhou Road. *Photograph by the author.*

13. China's Brave New World

I think you overestimate the danger of a "Brave New World"—i.e. a completely materialistic vulgar civilisation . . . the danger of that kind of thing is past. . . .

—A letter from George Orwell to Mr. S. Moos, December 1943 (Quoted in Bernard Crick, *George Orwell: A Life,* 1980)

I had to wait a long time before being able to embark on *Nineteen-Eighty Four.* Agreeing with all that the critics have written of it, I need not tell you how fine and how profoundly important the book is. . . .

[But whether] the boot-on-the-face [style of dictatorship it describes] can go on indefinitely seems doubtful. My own belief is that the ruling oligarchy will find less arduous and wasteful ways of governing and satisfying its lust for power, and that these ways will resemble those which I described in *Brave New World.* . . .

—A letter from Aldous Huxley to George Orwell, October 1949 (Quoted in Jeffrey Meyers, *Orwell: Wintry Conscience of a Generation,* 2000)

"Why couldn't they have picked *1984* instead?"

This was my first thought in August of 2002 when a faculty member from Heidelberg College, who had invited me to come speak at his Ohio campus, mentioned on the phone that all members of the school's entering freshman class had been assigned *Brave New World* as a core text. My reaction was not due to antipathy toward Aldous Huxley. On the contrary, when I was a teenager, I went through an avid Huxley phase, devouring not just his famous 1932 dystopian classic, but also some of his witty early novels and his 1954 book about mescaline, *The Doors of Perception.* Moreover, my interest in Huxley had recently been rekindled while doing research on Shanghai's past and present as a global city. This was because I found that Huxley was one of the many globetrotting intellectuals who visited that city early in the 1900s. Just a few months before that phone call, in fact, I had been leafing through Sybille Bedford's 1973 biography of the author searching (in vain as it turned out) for details on that Shanghai visit, about which Huxley wrote a wonderfully evocative short piece of reportage.

Why then, despite my fascination with Huxley, did I lament Heidelberg College's selection of *Brave New World* as a common reading for its several hundred incoming students? The main reason was simple. In addition to reading and talking about that novel, these same students were to start their academic year with a second common experience: watching *The Gate of Heavenly Peace,* a prize-winning documentary on the Chinese protests of 1989 directed by Carma Hinton and Richard Gordon. This was where my lecture came in, since I had worked on that Long Bow Group film as a consultant. The main reason for the August phone call was to finalize arrangements for my visit, and discuss the kind of talk I would give to place the 1989 protests and June 4th Massacre into perspective. And it is in this context that my response to the reference to *Brave New World* needs to be understood. My caller did not just tell me that the book had been assigned. He also mentioned casually that, though I should not feel compelled to do so, it would be wonderful if I could integrate some discussion of it into my lecture.

This seemed, at first, impossible. I could think of no obvious link between what I remembered from reading *Brave New World* almost thirty years previously—distracting futuristic movies called "feelies," a bliss-inducing drug called "soma," etc.—and the hunger strikes and bloodshed of China's 1989. By contrast, the June 4th killings and "Big Lie" campaign that followed—during which the regime insisted in classic Newspeak fashion (Orwell's fictional language that produced the slogan "War is Peace") that there had been no massacre, just a "riot" quelled with a minimum of violence by noble soldiers—cried out for Orwellian analysis. Surely, if China's 1989 showed anything, it was that "boot-on-the-face" policies were still flourishing fifty years after their imminent demise was predicted in the letter that Huxley wrote to Orwell (his one-time pupil at Eton)—a letter written, ironically, in the very month that the PRC was founded.

I had another secondary reason for regretting that *Brave New World*, not *1984*, had been chosen as a core reading: with the first anniversary of 9/11 approaching, Orwell seemed more directly relevant than Huxley to current events. When I socialized with faculty and students after my talk and conversation drifted to subjects in the news, I thought it would be difficult to bring up *Brave New World.* How much easier to refer to *1984* at a time when the White House was painting Iraq's leader as a "Big Brother" of the Persian Gulf and critics of Bush were hearing echoes of Newspeak in his rhetoric. If the people I interacted with were reading *1984* instead of *Brave New World,* I mused, it would even be easier to make small talk about television and films. After all, "Big Brother" was the name of a TV show earning high ratings in 2002, and there were strong Orwellian overtones to 1990s films such as *The Matrix* with which the incoming freshmen would be sure to be familiar.

When I hung up the phone that August, I put aside my disappointment and picked up the old copy of *Brave New World* that I had read long ago and had moved from apartment to apartment and house to house ever since without looking at its pages. And something curious happened: the more I read, the more I began to notice things that had quite a lot of relevance to contemporary concerns. I would like to pretend that everything fell neatly into place in time for me to turn my September lecture into a talk that moved seamlessly from China's 1989 to the stability-crazed, pleasure-mad society of the "Year of Our Ford 634" described by Huxley. That, however, would be an exaggeration. But I did manage to suggest some tentative connections between Huxley's most famous book and China's 1989 in my Ohio talk. And since then, as I have continued to ponder the issue, I have begun to see more links between *Brave New World* and contemporary concerns, Chinese and American alike, in part because of things that students and faculty members at Heidelberg College said to me during my visit.

Things have reached such a point, in fact, that I now wonder whether I got it all wrong back in 2002 when assessing the relative merits of assigning *Brave New World* as opposed to *1984*. To be sure, there is good reason to continue to read the latter, and it was fitting that in 2003, the centenary of the year in which Eric Blair (a.k.a. George Orwell) was born, it seemed that everyone was doing just that. It strikes me, though, that while 2003 was definitely Orwell's year, this might turn out in the end to be Huxley's century.

The main reason I say this has to do with my view on China, which I now think of as moving from a "*1984* Moment" at the time of Tiananmen into a "*Brave New World* Period," but recent developments in the United States show that the PRC is by no means the only country for which Huxley now provides an insightful guide. In retrospect, I have realized that one of the many things I was a bit mixed up about back in 2002 was the state of American popular culture. There is no question that the name of the show "Big Brother" (a program that originated in the Netherlands in 1999) is a nod to Orwell, and that the constant surveillance to which the contestants on that game show are subjected (variants of it are still showing in several countries, as I write this in early 2007) is straight out of *1984*. And yet, the vast majority of the people affected by the program are viewers being kept distracted and entertained. Shows such as this thus perform a function today that is not so far removed from that performed by the "feelies" in *Brave New World*.

Similarly, while there are things about *The Matrix* that are reminiscent of *1984,* there are probably even more echoes of Huxley than of Orwell to be found in its dialogue if one listens closely. After all, the central dilemma faced by more than one character is right out of *Brave New World*—choosing between a shallow life of sensual satisfaction combined with ignorance about how the world really works and a much more painful but self-aware form of existence. Another indication of Huxley's contemporary relevance has to do with the locations of cameras and screens in American luxury hotels.

Certainly, in the interests of security, patrons of such places are now being monitored more closely than in the past by surveillance systems (a point to Orwell). But a new trend is to include television screens in elevators (showing CNN, cartoons, or old "Three Stooges" films) to keep their temporary inhabitants happily distracted (score one for Huxley).

Turning to China, I now see 1989 as a turning point year when it comes to the relative weight that the regime has put on Orwellian as opposed to Huxleyan strategies. Make no mistake, Beijing is still capable at times of returning to "the boot-on-the-face," as shown periodically by the harsh treatment of Falun Gong sectarians, restive members of "ethnic minority" groups in Xinjiang and Tibet, workers attempting to found independent unions, and villagers angered by state policies, such as those shot by paramilitary forces in rural South China late in 2005. Nevertheless, to see China today as a Big Brother state is to miss much that has been going on in that country since 1989. This is because one big lesson that the regime took from the fall of state socialism in Europe was that, to stay in power, it needed to do a much better job at supplying those it governs with appealing material goods and forms of entertainment.

The Chinese Communist Party, to put this another way, began to embrace a strategy inspired as much by the soft authoritarianism of a Singapore as it was by the personality cult–style totalitarianism of a North Korea. Happiness through consumption began to be trumpeted more than salvation through personal self-denial, and stability was made the great watchword—just as Huxley imagined it would be in the "Year of Our Ford 634." Moves in the directions just described were afoot in China well before 1989: "To Get Rich is Glorious" became an official slogan early in the post-Mao era and floats showcasing attractive consumer goods began to appear in National Day parades. Such moves, though, have become more pronounced from the early 1990s onwards. And it is no surprise that the theme-parking of cities has moved forward swiftly in China as well as the United States in recent years, as urban spaces given over to entertainment are easier to square with Huxley's vision than Orwell's.

If I had to pick a single personal anecdote to illustrate the value of looking to Huxley even more than to Orwell for guidance when trying to come to terms with contemporary China, I would select my first visit to a Beijing internet café. This occurred in 1999, during the trip to the PRC that overlapped with the outbreak of anti-NATO protests. The visit to the internet café I have in mind took place on May 4, before the anti-NATO protests began, on the anniversary of a famous 1919 struggle, during which student protesters both castigated imperialist intervention in Chinese affairs and called for an end to corrupt and authoritarian governance at home. The May 4th Movement, as it is called, has a complex legacy: the Chinese government extols it as a glorious patriotic and revolutionary event, but dissidents in 1989 and other years have used its anniversary as a moment to criticize the regime, and to suggest that China's current rulers are no better than the warlords against whom students marched in 1919. One reason I went to the internet café was to see if I could find any traces in cyberspace of this being done on the 1999 anniversary date.

One thing I found out was that, not surprisingly, many of the obvious places to look for such evidence were blocked. This was proof that the Chinese government was trying, in Orwellian fashion, to limit the access that those it rules have to information that might contradict government lines. I soon discovered, though, that with a bit of creativity, I could circumvent these efforts. For example, while the *New York Times* site was blocked, many stories from that newspaper could be found simply by going to one of the many regional American newspapers that has its own web presence. Within five minutes, I was reading on one of those sites the text of a manifesto that had been written in China by a banned political group. I began to wonder if any of the Beijing youths in this internet café were doing the same thing, but I quickly became convinced that this was unlikely. As I glanced at the screens I passed as I wandered out of the building, I realized that far from looking for ways to get around Big Brother, most of its young patrons were indulging in one of the soma-equivalents of their generation: playing, in an enraptured state of bliss, an online video game. The soma comparison did not come to mind then: more interested in Habermas than Huxley, I thought of writing an essay called "What If They Built a Public Sphere and Nobody Came?" Now, though, I look back on that incident as a sign of just how far from *1984* and toward *Brave New World* the PRC had moved by 1999.

An internet café in Shanghai. *Photograph by the author.*

Does thinking of China in this way offer any clues as to what the future holds for the PRC? I am still too new to looking at the PRC through a Huxleyan lens to venture any definitive prognostication. I have, however, been struck by one possible future twist, which has to do with a *Brave New World* theme linked to literature.

One of the many ways in which Huxley imagined things would be different six centuries hence was that works once considered pornographic would be seen as unobjectionable, while works once considered canonical would be viewed as smut. Shakespeare's plays, for example, are banned in the society of *Brave New World,* while the "feelies," a form of art that makes D. H. Lawrence's steamiest novels seem tame, are officially endorsed. In China today, an equivalent kind of reversal has not taken place, but it is easy to suppose that it could. There has already been a dramatic shift as the regime allows many books once considered obscene or subversive to be sold. One can buy books about sex and treatises by Western liberal thinkers that would formerly have been banned. With social stability prized and high growth rates seen as the key to stability as well as a source of national pride, formerly taboo concepts relating to the economy are being integrated into government documents. And once forbidden foreign works are being studied for possible clues for helping to enrich individual Chinese and the Chinese nation as a whole. Even if they gained fame in part via their criticisms of Communism, this does not place Western writers beyond the pale.

When I mentioned this situation to a Soviet specialist colleague, he was intrigued and pressed me about what kinds of works remain off limits. Books about Tibet, I said, and about Taiwan, and works by Chinese dissidents. But, he asked, isn't there any Western writer viewed as dangerous? After thinking about this, one possibility came to mind—of someone who has not yet been banned but could be soon. His works stress that in a world of increasing disparities between rich and poor (like the PRC), it is good for the latter to band together against and make demands on the former, and that conflict, not stability, leads to progress. The Western thinker I have in mind is, of course, Karl Marx.

14. Chicago in an Age of Illusions

Theme parks—to modify the French anthropologist Levi Strauss's famous dictum about animals as used in totemic systems—are good to think. And recently scholars in various disciplines, from history and folklore to semiotics and sociology, have been thinking about them in interesting ways. So, too, have specialists concerned with very different parts of the world, from North America and Europe to Asia. The result has been insightful publications that limn theme parks proper (such as Disney's Magic Kingdoms) and the ur-theme parks of earlier times (such as International Expositions and World's Fairs), in an effort to illuminate the zeitgeists of particular moments in the history of capitalism and modernity. There have also been efforts by Sinologists and journalists interested in Asia to fill in the Chinese side of this global story. In his wonderful essay "The Garden of Perfect Brightness: A Life in Ruins," for example, Sinologist Geremie Barmé describes the theme-park-like elements of a famous Beijing site, which was laid out so that the country's Qing Dynasty rulers could take simulated tours of different parts of their realms without leaving the capital. And journalist Ian Buruma is among those who, in pieces such as "Asia World," have written about new Chinese theme parks, which feature everything from thrill rides to replicas of famous tourist attractions to dances and other sorts of performances by colorfully garbed representatives of *xiaoshu minzu* (ethnic minority groups). There are few writers who would describe their specialty as "theme park studies," but there is enough of a literature on the subject now to speak of it as comprising a burgeoning subfield, the impact of which has been particularly marked in certain cognate areas, such as urban studies and leisure studies.

Many of the foundational works on theme parks and related venues were published in the 1980s but continue to be read and debated. Tony Bennett's "The Exhibitionary Complex," which first appeared in the journal *New Formations* in 1988, is a case in point. So is Umberto Eco's *Travels in Hyperreality* and Jean Baudrillard's *Simulations,* the English translations of which both first appeared in 1987. In the 1990s, while influential single-author analyses continued to appear, some of the best works on theme parks and related issues started to be interdisciplinary collections. One of the most interesting works to appear during that decade was Neil Harris et al.'s lavishly illustrated *Grand Illusions: Chicago's World's Fair of 1893,* which was published to mark the centenary of an event that was attended by more than 27 million visitors and helped put what is now the Midwest's leading metropolis on the national (and global) map as a world-class urban center.

Another important publication of the 1990s remains my favorite collection on the topic: *Variations on a Theme Park: The New American City and the End of Public Space.* As someone with fond memories of childhood visits to Disneyland, and who later enjoyed taking his own children to that and other theme parks, such as Sea World in San Diego, some parts of that 1992 publication, edited by architect Michael Sorkin, seem unnecessarily dark. Some contributors are too focused for my taste on processes of control and manipulation, which are certainly part of the theme park story but by no means all of it. Even so, chapters such as those by M. Christine Boyer and Mike Davis, each of whom is always worth reading, are filled with insights. So, too, is "The World in a Shopping Mall," an essay by

Margaret Crawford that includes a good discussion of Chicago's Museum of Science and Industry, which is known in part for its simulated tour of a coal mine. Moreover, the book would be worth buying even if all it contained was the editor's wide-ranging closing chapter. This has fascinating things to say about everything from the theme-park dimensions of airports to the meaning of Chicago's 1893 expo and the even more heavily attended "Century of Progress" World's Fair held there forty years later.

As essays such as Crawford's and Sorkin's indicate, one recent trend has been an expansion within theme park studies of the sites deemed worthy of study. Increasingly, places other than geographically contained fairs and amusement centers have been subjected to the kind of analysis once reserved for locations like Coney Island or Sea World (the subject of an excellent study, *Spectacular Nature,* by folklorist Susan G. Davis). Multi-function mega-malls, heritage districts, even whole cities that have a spectacular air to them have become grist for the mill. Las Vegas alone has inspired several notable works. And why not? It has become a surreal place where you can dine near a half-scale Eiffel Tower, stroll by moonlight near a mock Pyramid, then retire to sleep in a room that has a view of a faux Lake Como.

As far as I know, turn-of-the-millennium Chicago has not yet been subjected to the city-as-theme-park treatment. But recent visits to it have left me convinced that there could hardly be a better candidate for it. To be sure, when it comes to blurring the line between real and virtual cities, it is no match for Las Vegas. It has too much concrete and steel, too many signs of economic activity unrelated to escapism, too many workers who are not misleadingly called by other names (such as the "cast members" at Disney World), for Chicago to be mistaken for anything but a real urban center. Still, in its current incarnation, it has plenty to offer scholars inspired by a Bennett or a Baudrillard.

Consider, first of all, Chicago's culinary landscape, which now includes a variety of theme-park-like restaurants. The Rain Forest Café, for example, where families can look at and listen to animatronic animals while they eat—an experience most reminiscent for me (having never been to the Amazon) of trips on the "Jungle Cruise" at Disneyland.

Or considers Chicago's stores, which have always lured window shoppers as well as purchasers of merchandise, but have not always gone as far as they do now to blur the line between consumption and entertainment. The famous "Magnificent Mile" shopping district on Michigan Avenue is dotted with stores that feel—at least a bit—like theme parks. Several contain high-tech arcade and video games, a few have mechanized displays and exhibits. One notable store of this sort is Nike Town, which has a Disney-ish name and combines exhibition (a pair of Michael Jordan's shoes are always on view) with fairground-style play (there is an indoor basketball court for customers to use). Another is the American Girl Place (website motto: "A Place for Smiles on the Magnificent Mile"), where customers can do much more than simply buy merchandise (from clothing to books) associated with a famous line of dolls (best known for ones linked to specific historical periods and representing distinctive ethnic or social groups). Inside its doors, young doll collectors (generally accompanied by both an adult and one of their dolls) can also have afternoon tea in the store's café or visit the store's theatre to see a show such as "The American Girls Revue" (website description: "Written by Broadway playwrights, this lively show brings the stories of the American Girls characters to life.")

Adding to the "shopping district as amusement park" effect are the varied ways you can break up a day spent along the Magnificent Mile. Tired of walking between stores? Journey between them in a horse-drawn carriage driven by a man (or, anachronistically, a woman) wearing Edwardian livery. Hungry but don't have time to go to the Rain Forest Café? Try the food court located high up in a building such as the Water Tower Place, an impressive structure known for its "vertical mall" shopping experience. Pick from the offerings at varied counters, each providing a taste of a different exotic (or not-so-exotic) cuisine (albeit the fast food variety of it), and head for a table by one of the big plate glass windows. From there, admire the parade of tiny shoppers who seem (from that height) like moving mannequins put on display for your viewing pleasure.

In addition, there are the museums. It is not just the Museum of Science and Industry that has its theme park elements. In the Field Museum, you can tour a model of an Egyptian tomb, then go on to

The American Girl Place in Chicago. *Photograph by Alan Thomas, used by permission.*

an exhibit on evolution that is cleverly built around mock "newscasts" on scattered television monitors ("mammals are becoming increasingly important at this stage in pre-history, details at 11:00"). And even one of its airports, O'Hare, has a theme park feel in one part—the long tunnel linking its B and C concourses, which provides a psychedelic neon light show for weary travelers with connections to make as they are carried along on moving walkways.

Last but not least, until it closed for business a few years ago, the city was home to a branch of "Disney Quest," an indoor theme park filled with arcade games and rides that made the most of what in the late 1990s constituted state-of-the-art virtual reality technologies. When this outlet first went into operation in 1999, in a prime location at 55 Ohio Street just east of the southern edge of the Magnificent Mile, it was one of only two places to go to if you wanted to experience the latest in high-tech wizardry that the world's biggest name in theme parks had to offer: Orlando, which was home to the original Disney Quest, was the other location. The Chicago Disney Quest was a Midwestern Magic Kingdom in a building, complete with several rides that involved sitting still but feeling as though you were traversing great distances via varied conveyances (a magic carpet, a river raft, and so on), thanks to the special effects provided by virtual reality goggles. The theme park's brochure, called an "Adventurer's Map," promised fun for children and adults alike and guaranteed all comers "five floors of virtual fun that put you in the middle of your favorite Disney adventures!"

With Disney Quest added to the mix, the problem became not deciding whether early-twenty-first-century Chicago deserved the full city-as-theme-park treatment but where best to turn for guidance in applying it. And this remains the case even though Disney Quest went out of business a few years ago. The difficulty for the analyst is that the literature on the topic of theme parks has grown so large and diverse that there are almost too many choices when it comes to places to begin. Some might still suggest taking one's cue from "The Exhibitionary Complex" and other essays by Bennett. These have the considerable virtue of demonstrating the relevance for theme park analysis of the insights of all three members of the current Holy Trinity of radical cultural analysis: Antonio Gramsci,

Michel Foucault, and Walter Benjamin. Other scholars, though, might prefer to point one elsewhere. Toward Eco, perhaps. Or toward *Variations on a Theme Park,* which has the attraction of connecting discussions of mega-malls and Magic Kingdoms to general commentaries on the urban condition by everyone from Émile Zola to Joan Didion, Jane Jacobs to Richard Sennett, David Harvey to William H. Whyte.

No matter where we begin, we are likely to find some articulation of a three-part evolutionary scheme, linking carnivals of the distant past to the Disney creations of the late twentieth century via the World's Fairs of the 1850s–1940s. In this scheme, the chaotic village fairs of the 1700s, the Crystal Palace Exhibition, and the first Magic Kingdom (which opened for business in California some fifty years ago) are presented as quite different, though related, landmarks. Put simply—much more simply than any theorist would actually put it—the idea is that the era of Mardi Gras inversions gave way to one of grand spectacle, and that in turn was superceded by the supposedly still current age of simulation.

In other words, so the story goes, first we had fairs dominated by local products, face-to-face exchanges between producers and consumers, simple amusements, and visions of ordinary hierarchies turned upside down. Then grand exhibitions that showcased goods from around the world and celebrated the futuristic potential of industry and technology came on the scene and ultimately began to dominate it. Here, clearer distinctions were made between participants and observers, that is, between those responsible for the displays and the spectators who were supposed to take in the spectacle and only incidentally contribute to it. Finally came sites built around fakes and facsimiles, where visitors were encouraged to suspend their sense of disbelief and imagine that they were seeing or hearing things that were not really there at all. The strolling spectator was replaced by an even more voyeuristic figure: the passive consumer of images, the person viewing life from aboard a people-mover, the temporarily mobile couch potato.

The lines between these stages in theme park history are always acknowledged to be blurry. Simulation was around long before Disneyland—in the form of wax museums, architectural follies, and many other things—and theorists readily admit this. They also do not pretend that recently built amusement parks have been stripped of all their spectacular vestiges. It makes sense to them that Disney World includes Epcot Center (with its exhibits of products from around the world), since circuses (performance equivalents to exhibitions) have continued to be enjoyed in the era of television (a media that depends heavily on the art of simulation). Moreover, while many of them stress that discipline and order have triumphed over subversive types of revelry as we have moved toward the present, few of the theorists I have in mind would claim that the spirit of carnival has been completely vanquished. And it would indeed be wrong to make that assertion. After all, as anyone can attest who remembers (as I do) the thrill of driving with a parent in the passenger seat on the Autopia ride at Disneyland, even in the most disciplined Magic Kingdom there is the potential for a Mardi Gras moment. What most analysts stress is that, as important as the overlaps between eras are, the strategy in a place like the Orlando park conglomeration is a complex set of tricks as opposed to carnival reversals—real objects tend to play second fiddle to marvels of artifice. In addition, they claim, there have been shifts in the ideal typical consumer of modernity and its pleasures. The haggler gave way to the nineteenth-century *flaneur* who in turn gave way to the private and passive consumer of images.

Where, then, does Disney Quest—whether in the form of the now-closed Chicago branch or still-open Orlando one—fit in? At first, it seems to be merely evidence that the era of simulation is now being taken to its logical (or illogical) conclusion. Many of the simulations are not of real places at all but rather of Disneyland attractions, which are themselves simulations. At Disney Quest, for example, at least in its Chicago incarnation, there was a "Virtual Jungle Cruise" ride in which you could go nowhere, but merely see a high quality computerized video projection as you paddled in a boat that rocked in imitation of the rapids you imagined yourself traversing. While you took your "adventure," you were simultaneously supposed to marvel at the virtual reality technology being deployed and, perhaps, think back to the last time you went on the "real" ride. And the closest thing to an exhibit hall was the "Midway

on the Moon" part of Disney Quest, which contained not agricul-
tural products of handmade wares, but rather arcade games from
different eras. These ran the gamut from simple ones in which you
roll a ball into a hole, to pinball and Pac Man, to the most recent virtual reality games that make you feel as though you are actually ski-
ing or shooting a gun at alien invaders.

This said, there is more to Disney Quest than the three-part evolutionary scheme of fair to exhibition to Disneyland can help us
grasp. We need, I think, to add in a fourth stage, while accepting, of
course, that once again there will be plenty of overlap and carry-over
from earlier periods. If the pre–Crystal Palace period was one of
Mardi Gras, while the 1850s–1940s was the era of grand spectacle,
and the last decades of the twentieth century were the age of simulation, a visit to Disney Quest suggested to me that we had just entered the time of participatory illusions.

Consider its high-tech versions of the roller coaster ride (a long-
time staple of amusement parks) and of a jousting match (a throwback to much earlier festive settings). At Chicago's Disney Quest,
before riding a coaster, you had to design one, choosing elements
from a computerized menu (a loop-the-loop here, a straight-away
section there). Then you entered a chamber and experienced a virtual reality version of this customized coaster. The joust match,
meanwhile, did not pit you against a flesh-and-blood opponent but
rather against comic book villains viewed through a virtual reality
visor. You tried to defeat these villains by waving a light saber that
came straight out of *Star Wars*.

Other sections of the park involved similar elements of cus-
tomization, participation, simulation, and structured creativity. In
an updating of the fun-house mirror, for instance, you could have a
snapshot taken of your face. This image then appeared in a mirror
before you and could be adjusted and modified in myriad ways of
your choosing. You could add a crown to your head, melt your chin,
add goblin ears—and then get a print-out of the new distorted you.

There was also a recording studio booth in which you could create a song and eventually burn your own CD working along similar
principles. You made a series of choices about musical and lyrical elements to include, the type of singer you want to hear singing, and

so forth. They gave you the framework for and list of possible titles and themes for the song—some of which had a carnival element, such as one called "I Need a Raise" that encourages adults to rant at their bosses, children to demand better treatment from their parents—and you filled in the details. It was a bit like karaoke, only you inserted yourself into the illusion not as a singer (though you could sometimes add a bit of your own voice) but rather as recording engineer, producer, and songwriter.

The karaoke singer is, come to think of it, a very good nominee for the successor to the *flaneur* and the couch potato in this era of participatory illusions. One thing that is appealing about it is that karaoke comes from Japan, which reflects the way that we are seeing—in this latest stage of theme park history—geographical conventions turned inside out and upside down. In nineteenth-century exhibitions, after all, the most "primitive" objects typically came from places outside the West such as Asia. On the Midway to the Moon, by contrast, it tends to be the most as opposed to least sophisticated arcade games that come from the other side of the Pacific.

In addition, geographical points of origin become even more slippery on the World Wide Web (the ultimate twenty-first-century theme park?), which is where we find many new examples of participatory illusions (such as chat rooms). Enter a virtual cocktail party in cyberspace, and you have no way of knowing where the next person you "meet" is actually based. Your interlocutor could be sitting in an internet café in Beijing or Bangkok, logging on from Madrid or the Millennium Dome.

Once upon a time, the person in question could even be interacting with you from Chicago's Disney Quest, which had computer terminals located near the Midway on the Moon. At these terminals, your on-screen guide, helping you to navigate the through-the-looking-glass environment of the web, was the Cheshire Cat—modeled, of course, not on drawings in any book but on the Disney film version of *Alice in Wonderland.*

So, what does it mean that Chicago's Disney Quest closed midway through 2001? Was its failure to turn a big enough profit a sign that the era of participatory illusions was already giving way to something still newer? I think not. I say this not just because the main reason it lost money may have been that the prices it charged were a bit too steep, and that too many Midwestern families turned out to be happy to go to Orlando when seeking a Disney experience.* And not just because other Chicago businesses with some similar features, such as the ESPN Zone and the American Girl Place, seem to be doing fine.

What it seems to me the demise of Disney Quest may, in fact, have represented was not the waning but the further assertion of the hold of the era of participatory illusions. Anyone who lives in or regularly visits Chicago and can afford a fast computer no longer needs to pay an admission fee to partake in Disney Quest–like adventures. There are now plenty of computer games (some marketed by Disney) that provide a host of karaoke-style forms of audio and visual entertainment. And with games such as Sim Theme Park readily available for use on home computers and laptops, anyone can build and ride a virtual roller coaster without waiting in line for the opportunity.

---

* According to a July 8, 2001, report in the *Milwaukee Journal Sentinel*, accessed via Lexis/Nexis on January 28, 2006, the only reason the company gave for the closing was that the Chicago franchise "wasn't making enough money."

15. Why Go Anywhere?

GET OUT NOW. Not just outside, but beyond the trap of the programmed electronic age so gently closing around so many people. . . . Outside lies unprogrammed awareness that at times become directed serendipity. Outside lies magic.

These are the sentences that open and close the first cluster of paragraphs in *Outside Lies Magic: Regaining History and Awareness in Everyday Places,* a wonderful book by John R. Stilgoe, a professor of landscape history at Harvard. His slim volume (187 pages of text) is a rare combination of whimsy and erudition, and is filled with intriguing suggestions of simple ways to rediscover the excitement of exploring ordinary sites—exploration of a sort that Stilgoe says should be thought of as a forgotten and underappreciated "liberal art" that can liberate the mind and also be fun. The book's cover features several black-and-white shots and one color photograph of a bicycle, a vehicle that Stilgoe claims provides one of the two best modes of travel (the other being walking) for "explorers" of the sort he calls on his readers to become. Slow methods of transport, he insists, are necessary if one is to engage in the kind of rumination on everyday objects (from telephone wires to soda cans) that can help us re-enchant and reach a new appreciation for the world around us.

I only became aware of Stilgoe's guide to unguided exploration quite recently, when it was brought to my attention by Tom Gieryn, an Indiana University sociologist with whom I once taught a graduate course on the enduringly local dimensions of even the most global cities. Knowing how my mind works, he pulled it from his shelves and handed it to me as soon as I mentioned that I was considering writing a piece for this book that would ask why international travel, even to settings that have supposedly been thoroughly Americanized, can still be full of encounters with the unexpected and the surprising.

At first it seemed the wrong book to have given me, so different were some of the moves I was planning to make in that imagined piece—which has now become this real one—from those that Stilgoe makes in *Outside Lies Magic*. For example, he calls on his readers to turn off their televisions. By contrast, one of the things that I planned to encourage my readers to do was to turn on the sets in their hotel rooms as soon as they arrived in a foreign country—just to see how long it took them to find a show that looked familiar in some ways, yet very strange in others. They might not always be as lucky as I was in Tokyo in 2004, when I began flipping channels and ended up watching what I soon realized (even with language skills so rusty as to be almost non-existent) was a rendition of a classic episode of *I Love Lucy*, done completely in Japanese with Japanese actors and actresses (the mannerisms of the actor who played "Ricky" and the pitch-perfect wail of the actress channeling Lucille Ball gave away the source). More generally, while Stilgoe's focus is on things you can do close to home, mine was to be on experiences one can only get from venturing far afield. You can get where he wants you to go by strolling or biking, but the "explorers" I had in mind needed to take jets.

Still, as I read through the book and thought about it, I realized that Tom had been right to give it to me. It probably was just the right thing to help me sharpen my thinking about the piece I had described in vague terms to him. This is because just as Stilgoe's book provides readers with suggestions about trying to go about looking at their surroundings in new ways, my goal here is to describe some techniques that international travelers can use—or really games they can play (like the "Turn the television on and commence to channel surf" one just described)—to make themselves more keenly aware of just how different from one another the major cities of Europe, Asia, and Australia continue to be from their American counterparts. This is true even of places that seem to have as many Starbucks outlets and Seven Eleven stores as Chicago; have freeway overpasses like those associated with L.A.; have skyscrapers designed by architectural firms that do business in New York; have bookstores that stock as many copies of the latest Harry Potter adventure as a Boston branch of Borders; and have teenagers who seem to (and might be) wearing the exact same fashions and using the exact same cell phones as their age-mates in Savannah and San Francisco.

Today explorers must teach themselves lessons of visual acuity long absent from grammar schools and universities, and they can learn only by looking hard. . . . The explorer notices and ponders. . . .
—John R. Stilgoe, *Outside Lies Magic*

Back-tracking a bit, I should note where the inspiration to write this piece came from in the first place. It all began with my first visit to Australia, which took place in July of 2005. The reason for the trip was to moderate a roundtable on human rights that was part of the International Congress of Historical Sciences—or what I called the "History Olympics" because the gatherings only take place once every five years (not quite an Olympic cycle, but close enough); scholars take part as members of national delegations, almost like teams; and that particular one was being held in Sydney, a city tightly linked in the minds of many with the 2000 Games. (Lest the term come across as hopelessly arrogant as opposed to playful, whenever I told people I would soon be heading to the "History Olympics," I was quick to point out a couple of key difference between these academic "international games" and the athletic variety: for example, that one did not have to be exceptionally talented to make the "team," just be part of a panel or roundtable proposal that got accepted or be on one of the organization's committees.)

When I got to the conference, I was struck by the fact that several historians I knew, who like me had come to Australia for the first time for this conference, expressed regret that Sydney seemed much like other Western (and particularly, American) cities they had been to before. So much so as to be of only limited interest to them. Sure, they admitted, the beaches were beautiful and so was the weather (even though it was winter), and the Opera House and Sydney Harbour Bridge were wonderfully photogenic. But unless one had time to get into the outback (something most of them could not do, as their schedules or financial situation or both were such that they would have to head home almost as soon as the conference was over), a trip to Sydney just didn't seem likely to supply the sort of kick that being in a truly exotic setting could provide them.

My own response to Sydney was quite dissimilar, veering much more toward that of some of my other colleagues, who found the city to have enough special qualities that even if one was confined to its central districts, one could get the frisson of being in a place unlike any one had been to before. By midway through the conference, in fact, I had compiled a long list of things I had seen (including various plants and trees filled with bats near the heart of a metropolis) or heard (beginning with the sounds of some birds) in the city that had no counterpart in any American or European city I had ever visited. I have to admit, though, that when I checked into my first Australian hotel, and noticed that there was a branch of the Subway sandwich franchise right next door, I had a momentary feeling of just the sort of ennui—a feeling that the world had shrunk far too much and far too quickly, so that it might soon not be worth the bother of going abroad unless one absolutely had to—that those participants in the History Olympics who had been disappointed by Sydney's lack of sufficient otherness had described.

Admittedly, Subway has never achieved the sort of status as a symbol of rampant Americanization that KFC and the Golden Arches have enjoyed (if that is the right word), but to me catching sight of a branch near my Sydney hotel was more disturbing than seeing a giant likeness of Colonel Sanders or Ronald McDonald. One of the early-twenty-first-century pop culture claims to fame of Bloomington, Indiana, where I was living in 2005, after all, was that a local man, who had lost a lot of weight on a diet largely composed of certain kinds of Subway sandwiches, had become the company's main television spokesman. In addition, a week or so before heading to Australia, I had been in Homer, Alaska, on a family trip, and the closest fast food outlet to the condo we had stayed in (indeed, the only fast food restaurant in the wharf area that is a hub of shopping, tourist, and fishing activity in Homer) had been a branch of Subway. To think that one could go from near the North Pole to near the South Pole and cross the Pacific to boot, yet still be within easy reach of a sandwich-making chain with an Indiana connection—well, it gave me an odd sense of vertigo. Had the feeling stayed with me, a piece inspired by Australia would have had a very different title than this one, perhaps "The Subway at the Edge of the Universe," and been very different in tone.

Ironically, one of the sights that put me solidly in the "Syndey is a place filled with curious novelties if you look hard enough" camp was another restaurant that at first, but only at first, seemed as though it had been magically transported straight from an American city. The eatery was called "Cheers," and it did not simply share a name with the eponymous bar of the long-running American sit-com set in Boston. It had a façade and used a style of lettering and a color scheme that were all clearly intended to remind passersby of the locale where the former baseball star Sam Malone (Ted Danson) mixed drinks and the acerbic Carla (Rhea Perlman) waited tables. But a closer examination of the outside of the establishment (the sort of scrutiny Stilgoe encourages his readers to give every store-front on a smalltown main street) revealed something surprising: this "Cheers" served a variety of curries and noodle dishes. It did not offer bar snacks like its Boston namesake, just Thai food. And later, when I took the time to "notice and ponder," rather than hurry along, I discovered, on the street on which my hotel and that Subway outlet stood, that the same was true of the "Malibu" restaurant. I had passed it by without stopping to examine the menu the first time I walked that stretch of road, even though I was in search of someplace to eat dinner. Why? I was in the mood for spicy food and mistakenly assumed that this eatery with its California name would serve salads and maybe burgers, not the kinds of hot dishes I craved.

Exploration encourages creativity, serendipity, invention.
So read this book, then go.

—John R. Stilgoe, Outside Lies Magic

My experiences with restaurants did not lead me down the road to thinking up games for world travelers—games designed in part to help reveal as an illusion that there are cities outside of the United States that have been so thoroughly Americanized as to be uninteresting to the frequent traveler. No. What pushed me in that direction was doing something simple that I always try to do whenever I am on my own in a foreign country: find a locally produced newspaper in a language I can read, buy it, and read it with my morning coffee. I do this partly because reading a newspaper while drinking coffee is a comforting morning ritual, partly to keep up with world affairs, partly in hope of learning something about the place I am spending time.

Very early in my week-long stay in Australia, playing out this ritual took me to the "Travel" section of the July 2–3, 2005, weekend edition of the *Sydney Morning Herald*. And it was there that I came upon a story by Jordan Baker called "Into a Surreal World," which was accompanied by an eye-catching illustration of a man with dice for eyes about to throw a dart at a map (or himself, it is hard to tell). The story began with this provocative teaser: "Been there, done that? Then put on your horse's head and get ready for a bizarre journey." The main focus of the article was the publication of a new book, Joel Henry and Rachel Antony's *The Lonely Planet Guide to Experimental Travel*. The goal of the book was apparently to "help readers become more receptive to the nuances" of cities they visited, so that they "noticed things they might otherwise have ignored." I was intrigued by this notion, but felt that some of the suggested "games" described in the article were of little use to the business traveler who needed to be in a particular city at a particular time, did not want to make elaborate preparations, yet wanted to be helped to "get more out of new places," one of the main aims of "experimental travel" as described in the article.

I began to muse on "games" that could be played in any locale, without advance planning, in short snatches of time (breaks of a few hours in the midst of conferences, while waiting for a plane connection) and could be played solo (though comparing results with other players might be even better). No doubt, as Lonely Planet publications tend to be practical, the actual book had some of these. But those described in the article seemed too elaborate or contrived ("hitchhiking in Strasbourg with 'Bora Bora, Tahiti' written on a sign"), or to require more time and flexibility in terms of choice of destination than I was likely to have. So, I came up with the following alternatives:

Game 1: Lost in Translation

> Explorers quickly learn that exploring means sharpening all the senses, especially sight.
>
> —John R. Stilgoe, *Outside Lies Magic*

This game is very basic and has, in a sense, already been introduced via the comments above about Sydney eateries and an *I Love Lucy* episode showing up when I flipped my television set on in Japan. In a nutshell, the object is to be on the lookout for things that seem in part just like, but in part totally unlike something with which you are familiar. Seeing a "Cheers" menu featuring Pad Thai is one sort of case in point, while listening to a Japanese actor try to evoke the most famous version of a Cuban accent ever heard on an American sitcom is another kind. (For the record: if I had stumbled onto an actual re-run episode of *I Love Lucy*, in English, I would have just kept flipping stations and not counted it as a find, even if it had Japanese subtitles running along the bottom of the screen, as this would be too small an alteration to matter.)

Naming this game after the Sofia Coppola film about a jet-lagged Bill Murray who has gone to Japan to make a Suntory Whiskey commercial seems particularly appropriate—for one generic reason and two more personal ones. The generic reason is that the game can be played, is perhaps actually best played, when strung out by jet lag (especially the version of it that requires no movement beyond hitting the button of a remote control). The first, more personal reason (which almost led me to call the game "In Taipei, It's Always Suntory Time") has to do with all-night convenience stores. In Taiwan, there are Seven Eleven franchises that look from the outside just like their U.S. counterparts, but if you look harder, examine the shelves carefully like a Stilgoe explorer, you will find unexpected things: underwear, XO Cognac, and, yes, Suntory Whiskey.

The second more personal reason why a film set in Japan seems particularly apt to link to the name of this game is that the *I Love Lucy* episode was not the only sight I saw in that country that made me conscious of the curious things that can happen when iconic people or objects move between cultures. There was also my visit to the Tokyo Tower. Modeled on the Eiffel Tower, but pointedly built to be just a bit taller (333 meters to the 320 of its Parisian inspiration) so that it could claim (as its official website does) to be the "world's tallest self-supporting steel structure," it was erected in 1958. When I visited it, I saw no other American tourists there—something that immediately sets it apart from its Parisian counterpart (and suggested that this tower is not high on the itinerary of international travelers, at least not those coming from the West). But there are other things altered in translation as well, beginning with the fact that the lower sections of the Tokyo Tower are filled with things that would seem totally out of place in a comparable part of the Eiffel Tower, such as an "Aquarium" (with 50,000 fish according to the website) and a "Carnival" section (that includes both a "Mysterious Walking Tour" enlivened by "hologram technology" and a wax museum that features "lifelike" representations of "fairy-tale" characters and popular entertainers—the website shows two of the Beatles). The Tokyo Tower presents itself as being like the Eiffel Tower but more modern: not only does the website boast of its greater height, but also its lighter weight, "about 4,000 tons" as opposed to 7,000 tons, the result of "a remarkable advance in steel manufacturing and construction technology." And yet, the overall effect of the Tokyo Tower is of a place that seems as much a throwback to earlier eras of spectacle (wax museums were the rage in Paris well before the Eiffel Tower went up in 1889) as it is a symbol of the technological advances of the contemporary era.

For Americans who have lived abroad at some point, as opposed to simply taking short trips to foreign countries, there is an interesting variation on this game to play. The trick here is to try to look at sites (even ones in your hometown) the way that they might be looked at by a friend of yours from the foreign country in which you once lived. It is worth reversing one's gaze in this way periodically, simply to remind yourself that it is not just when things are "translated" from the United States to other places that much is "lost" or reshaped in transit.

Food, once again, is an obvious place to start. Having lived in China, it is fascinating to eat in Chinese restaurants in the United States (and other countries) and see how much or little the experience resembles spending time in an eatery in Beijing or Canton. Some dishes show up everywhere (or nearly everywhere) but there are often intentional and unintentional variations relating to how ingredients are used, the order dishes are served, and so on. It is surely no more strange for an American traveler to find Thai food at the "Malibu" in Sydney, or discover that a Parisian eatery with "Indiana" in its name specializes in Tex-Mex dishes, than for a Chinese traveler to learn that in L.A. the soup is served first (not last); Kungpao chicken (*gongbao jiding*) comes with vegetables mixed in (it never does in Sichuan restaurants on the other side of the Pacific); and banquets are accompanied by lots of rice (an everyday food considered too ordinary to be a significant part of a fancy meal in Nanjing) and curious objects called "fortune cookies" (a North American invention). A there-to-here example of much being lost in translation that does not relate to food involves the image of Ernesto "Che" Guevara. In Key West, as I discovered during a family trip there, Che signifies Cuba as a place, more than revolution. This makes it seem natural, as it would not in Latin America, for Che and Hemingway (Ernesto and Ernest) t-shirts and caps to be displayed side-by-side in local shops for tourists.

Game 2: Entering the Time Tunnel

> Any contemporary explorer who deserts the paved road for the roadbed footpath moves into a time tunnel. . . . Everything within the leafy corridor, or within the grassy corridor separating pastures and arable fields, once crackled with the highest tech of all . . . and here and there the explorer of ruins discerns the remnants of technology decayed.
>
> —John R. Stilgoe, *Outside Lies Magic*

This game, which is also simple (and shares a name with the television show), involves a reversal of one of Stilgoe's claims: that paying attention to what was once high tech but is now passé can enrich an explorer's sense of everyday environments. There are plenty of "ruins" in any city, of course, and wandering in them can provide the sort of "time tunnel" experience that Stilgoe has in mind. But there are also unusual objects to encounter in such cities that might or might not be the next big thing technologically, and this game encourages you to first imagine yourself being beamed ten years into the future, and then ponder whether these objects have become commonplace or relics. Will all major cities of the future have these things that seem novelties when you encounter them in one place today? Will they have remained distinctive to that particular place? Or will they simply have disappeared?

I saw the first objects that made me pose these questions in Tokyo in 2004, though I would not consider the possibility of making them part of a game until a year later. What I saw in Japan's capital was a streetside vending machine—or, rather, hundreds of such machines, which are ubiquitous in the heart of Tokyo. There are plenty of Starbucks in Japan's capital, as stories about runaway globalization often note in passing, but until my 2004 visit to that city, I had no idea just how much easier it was to get a caffeine fix in a hurry there than in any American or European metropolis I have visited. You may never have to walk more than a block or two before hitting a café in Paris or a coffee shop in New York's downtown. In addition, some individual blocks in the heart of those two urban centers may have several different places to stop in for an espresso or cup of coffee. This is nothing, though, compared to Tokyo, where there are just as many cafés and coffee shops—plus at least as many vending machines out on the streets ready to instantly dispense a cold coffee drink. Was this my first spotting of a trend that will soon spread to all global cities? I still haven't made up my mind, but it is interesting to ponder. And if I were a truly organized traveler and player of this game, I would write "2004 Tokyo streetside coffee machines" on a slip of paper, place the words "trend" and "dead-end" beside the phrase, circle one, seal the guess in an envelope marked "do not open until 2020," file it away, and then pull it out again when the appropriate time came to see if I was right.

There was one object I encountered in Sydney, which was by no means ubiquitous (I just noticed it in the lobby of one hotel), that can be subjected to the same treatment. This was a machine that gave users the option of swiping their credit card and, in return, getting a print-out of that day's issue of any one of a dozen or so different newspapers. I wasn't tempted to swipe my card, in part because, as already noted, I like to read local newspapers while I travel. Still, I could see the appeal for certain kinds of travelers, such as those who were homesick or simply wanted to follow a story that would not be covered in an Australian newspaper.

I am not an organized enough player of this game to write down my guesses—and one nice thing about all of these games, I think, is that you do not have to be an organized player and can feel free to write nothing down and to stop and start playing them at will. Still, if I were organized, I'd probably circle "trend" for the Tokyo vending machines and "dead-end" for the Sydney newspaper dispenser (even though it did come with a cute picture on the front of it showing a happy dog with a newspaper in his mouth). After all, the desire for ever-speedier ways to satisfy a caffeine-craving seems to have the potential to keep growing, whereas laptop computers and wireless connections are making it easier and easier to get to the website of your favorite newspaper quickly and efficiently wherever you are.

This Time Tunnel game need not have a purely technological focus, as it can be interesting to speculate whether other things, seen for the first time abroad, represent a sense of things to come or something that will remain in place only outside of the United States or disappear completely in time. For example, on a 2005 stay in Turku, Finland, which I had come to in order to serve as external examiner for a doctoral defense, I noticed two things I had never seen before. First, in my room at the Scandic Hotel, which is part of the Hilton organization, there was a trash can divided into sections, so that the environmentally concerned guest could put recyclable materials in one part, other kinds of trash in another. Trend or dead-end?

Second, while walking through a local department store, I

noticed a line of giant posters for a line of clothing that showed young women dressed fashionably (nothing unusual) standing in front of striking-looking buildings (again, hardly a novelty). What was arresting to me about the posters was that the cityscape displayed was not that of Paris, New York, Milan, or Tokyo. Instead, it was Pudong (East Shanghai), the buildings of which I had previously only seen integrated into advertisements within Asia. Trend or dead-end? I wish I could say that I expect hotel rooms in North America to soon have the eminently sensible "green" trash cans I saw in Turku, but I feel more confident about the global proliferation of advertisements featuring futuristic Pudong skyscrapers.

Game 3: Follow the Bouncing Icon

> Exploring as I teach it depends heavily on understanding the pasts that swirl around any explorer of ordinary landscape . . . I emphasize that the built environment is a sort of palimpsest, a document in which one layer of writing had been scraped off, and another one applied. An acute, mindful explorer who holds up the palimpsest to the light sees the earlier message. . . .
> —John R. Stilgoe, *Outside Lies Magic*

This game, which has to do with trying to appreciate one particular way that contemporary cities can be read as palimpsests, is another that I thought up in Australia in 2005. But its inspiration and the roots of its name lie in a wonderfully conceived interdisciplinary workshop on "urban icons" held in Los Angeles at the University of Southern California the preceding year. The workshop's structure was simple: bring together a group of people in different fields, ranging from Classics and geography to film studies and history, and ask them to take part in discussions about the objects or people that have become readily understood shorthands for specific cities (the way that the Eiffel Tower is for Paris, the Golden Gate Bridge is for San Francisco, and so on) and reflect on how these "urban icons" rise and fall, change their meaning, or are represented in novel ways and through new media over time. The gathering was memorable both for smart presentations and lively conversations, and for the way the overall experience was enhanced by meals eaten at iconic structures, one working definition of which is the sort of places that show up on postcards.*

Some good conferences launch new research projects, but that one triggered a new travel obsession—keeping track of the myriad ways that representations of iconic buildings, modes of transportation, and so on are used. Within a city, for example, they are sometimes deployed to remind you of where you are, or to convince you that the metropolis you are spending time in is in the same league as the most renowned urban centers on earth. Another thing interesting to track while traveling is the way that a contemporary icon has been displaced or is being used together with representations of things that in an earlier time stood for that metropolis.

To give a sense of what I have in mind, consider the case of the two Shanghai icons that were the subject of my paper for the L.A. conference: the clock-towered Customs House that stands on the western bank of the Huangpu River and the space-needle-like Pearl of the Orient Tower that stands across the water from it in Pudong (and is one of the buildings that was featured in the billboards inside the Turku department store). When I returned to Shanghai a few months after the workshop, in July of 2004, my concern with tracking the uses and rise and fall of these two icons was taken to new extremes, as I was determined to judge the current state of play in the relationship between the pair of buildings. In my conference paper (since revised and published in the Cambridge University Press journal *Urban History,* as part of a special issue co-edited by conference organizers Vanessa Schwartz and Philip Ethington), I had focused in part on the rivalry for iconic supremacy between the Customs House (built in the mid-1920s) and its Pudong competitor, the Pearl of the Orient Tower, from the latter's 1995 creation until 2002.

---

* The most notable such meal was a dinner at Case Study House 22, a 1958 home that the *Los Angeles Times* (October 7, 2004) has called "a glass-walled miracle in the Hollywood Hills." A creation of architect Pierre Koenig, the house is the subject of a famous photograph by Julius Shulman, which has been reproduced on many postcards. Adding to its iconicity has been the way its swimming pool and interior have been featured in various films (*Nurse Betty, Galaxy Quest,* etc.) with scenes set in Los Angeles.

Thus, as I walked off the plane during my 2004 return visit, I had my camera ready to snap as many images as I could of representations of either or both buildings (they often show up together, sometimes along with other waterfront landmarks, on guidebook covers and maps—two things that, like postcards and establishing shots used in films, are key indexes of iconicity).

I didn't have to wait long to take my first shot, since the first poster I saw inside the terminal itself showed the radio and television tower, standing for Shanghai, flanked by a series of famous urban icons, from London's Big Ben to Sydney's Opera House. And by the end of my first day in the city, I had taken photographs of scores of representations of both the Pearl of the Orient Tower and the Customs House, sometimes shown on their own, sometimes shown together, often shown in the company of other buildings of similar vintage near them, such as the Jinmao Tower (home to the "highest hotel on earth") in the case of the Pudong icon, the art deco Peace Hotel in the case of the Puxi (West Shanghai) one. And the pattern continued during the following days.

Had I been a thorough collector of iconic memorabilia, moreover, I would have ended the trip needing a new piece of luggage in which to store new acquisitions related to one or both of these buildings, ranging from coffee table books to posters, Pearl of the Orient Tower thermometers to sepia-toned framed reproductions of old photographs of the Bund, showing the Customs House standing beside its next door "elder brother," the domed Hong Kong and Shanghai Bank building. One of the lightest items in that new suitcase would have been a pair of special postcards available within the city's Urban Planning Museum. These are issued by a machine, with a built-in camera, that allows purchasers to incorporate photographs of themselves onto a card with a pre-set background (one option included the Pearl of the Orient Tower, another the Customs House) before it pops out. (A perfect example of a souvenir for the age of "participatory illusions," but one might ask of this machine—trend or dead end?)

There are no clearly spelled out rules to "Follow the Bouncing Icon" (making this game just like the others in this regard). The basic goal is simply to assess what the main current icon for a city is; see how varied the uses to which it is being put are; and, after figuring

An advertisement for a Hong Kong development company displayed in the Pudong Airport. *Photograph by the author.*

out whether there was something that stood for the urban center before the iconic flavor of the month was created or gained prominence, pondering how easy or difficult in this case it is to get a sense of earlier visual grammars for representing the metropolis. This last aspect of the game can be prepared for in advance by doing things like searching out an old guidebook to a city before heading there to see, for example, what the first illustration in such a work dealing with Paris was before Eiffel built his tower in 1889.*

It is not necessary to do any advance preparation, though, as getting into a conversation with local residents about what they consider the most prominent symbol for their city and whether something else played that role in the past will do the trick. Such conversations can quickly clue you in about alternatives and competitors to whatever seems, in the international sphere, to be the city's reigning contemporary icon. Asking the same question of locals of different generations may be particularly useful, and it is the kind of conversation that is easy to have with shopkeepers, waitresses, people sitting near you at internet cafés, and so forth.

Here are two things about icons worth pondering after arriving in a city. Of course there will be t-shirts, postcards, guidebooks, key rings, maps, and so on, but are there less expected places that images show up of the reigning current icon or of both past and present icons of the particular metropolis you are in? Is it possible to stroll several blocks down a main thoroughfare and *not* see any representations of its main icon or icons—something it is now very hard to do in Shanghai, so omnipresent are billboards, phone cards, advertisements and so on that include images of the most famous buildings that line one or both sides of the Huangpu River?

Sydney turned out to be a good place to play this particular game,

---

* Travelogues can also be useful here: Twain's *Innocents Abroad* suggests, for instance, that the Louvre and Notre Dame were key icons for Paris before the Eiffel Tower went up—and was decried by some Parisians as a monstrosity that had destroyed the look of their metropolis, the same thing some Shanghainese have said about the Pearl of the Orient Tower. Of course, even after the Eiffel Tower became the most iconic site in Paris, it did not exert a complete monopoly over guidebook covers and the like, as one sometimes finds tourist materials that feature the Louvre, and the Pudong airport poster mentioned above used the Arc de Triomphe to stand for the French capital.

due to the abundance of settings in which the Opera House shows up—and the fact that, due to their proximity, this icon and its most important predecessor, the Harbour Bridge, often show up together in photographs. During my first days in Sydney, I did not think much about the Harbour Bridge, so much did the Opera House stand out as *the* iconic local site—just as it is *the* main thing that people outside of Sydney associate with the metropolis. Prior to visiting Sydney, I was primed to see its image everywhere. With some cities (Los Angeles, for example) there is no single building that shows up on most guidebook covers and maps. With other cities, a traveler from America is unlikely to have strong images beforehand of any particular local site, as was the case with me when I first visited Helsinki in 2006. Sydney, though, did not fall into either of these categories. Every guidebook I looked at in advance had the Opera House on its front, and on that Shanghai airport billboard and other similar representations of Iconic Line-ups (as they might best be called) that I had seen in Asia, the Opera House was as sure to be there standing for Sydney as Big Ben was sure to be there standing for London.*

Though I was thus prepared to see a great many representations of the Opera House in Sydney, just *how* unavoidable its image turned out to be took me aback. At the History Olympics, for example, not only did the program every participant was given have the Opera House on its cover, but there was a miniaturized version of the same image on the badges with our names and country (reinforcing the sense of being part of a national "team") that we were given and encouraged to wear. And the same image appeared as well on the bags that we were given to carry around our materials. Looking out at the audience during the session I chaired, my eyes were thus confronted with people wearing tags with the Opera House on

---

* Not surprisingly, iconic line-ups may be especially important where new buildings, just establishing their claim to fame, are concerned. Consider the case of Taipei 101. In the mall that takes one up the initial floors of that recently built edifice, iconic line-ups, which visually link the skyscraper you are in to famous old structures associated with other cities, seem to be everywhere. Such images even make up the background for special Taipei 101 credit cards and appear on the free shopping bags offered those who sign up for one of these credit cards.

them, leafing through programs with Opera House covers, and having at their side or in front of them satchels emblazoned with the Opera House. The effect was not unlike that created by fun house mirrors.

So prevalent was the Opera House's image that it was easy to slip into thinking of Sydney as lacking the palimpsest quality Stilgoe stresses, or the dueling icons quality that I had been tracking in regard to Shanghai. But on a side trip to Canberra, to give a talk at Australia National University on my Shanghai icons work, I realized that I had been missing something important. During my Canberra presentation, I made a passing comment about having been struck by just how omnipresent images of the Opera House had seemed to me in Sydney, and how that city had seemed one in which there was an unusually simple iconic story to tell. During the question and answer session that followed, though, a leading China specialist who had grown up in Sydney set me straight on the status of the Opera House: though internationally far more widely recognized, some local people remained far more attached to the Harbour Bridge as a symbol for the city.

Upon returning to Sydney, I played a variation of the "Follow the Bouncing Icon" (all of these games invite the player to improvise versions).* In this version, my goal was to count the number of times that visual representations of the Opera House showed the Harbour Bridge as well. (Half turned out to do this, but it was easy for the outsider—though perhaps much less so the locals, especially those old enough to remember a city without the former—to assume that the latter was the less significant structure in such

---

* There is a variation I made up later that helps while away time waiting for United connections in Chicago's O'Hare airport. At each gate (and this is true in San Francisco at SFO and perhaps other airports), United has a display screen that alternately shows you the name of the place a flight is bound and an object associated with that destination. The trick is to see if, upon seeing the place name, you can guess the icon. Sometimes it's easy—St. Louis is represented by its famous Arch—but sometimes it is tricky. Is San Francisco represented by the expected Golden Gate Bridge? No, by a Cable Car. And what about L.A.? Is it represented by a) a freeway cloverleaf, b) the Hollywood sign, c) the Beverly Hills Hotel, or d) none of the above? To find out, just go find the gate of an LAX-bound plane the next time you are delayed at O'Hare.

shots.) It was interesting to note rare cases (such as the website for the University of New South Wales, which was the first thing I saw each time I logged on to check e-mail during the conference) that featured the Harbour Bridge but not the Opera House. And to note a parallelism in suggested tourist itineraries, which encouraged visitors to tour the Opera House and then later, if they had the nerve and money, pay to be part of a group climbing excursion to the top of the Harbour Bridge.

Game 4: Global Moments and Worldly Places

> Any explorer sees things that reward not just a bit of scrutiny but a bit of thought, sometimes a lot of thought over the year. Put the things in spatial context or arrange them in time, and they acquire value immediately.
>
> —John R. Stilgoe, *Outside Lies Magic*

This final game was inspired by, of all things, a baggage carousel. More precisely, the one I stood by when I finally arrived in the Sydney airport after the last of a series of planes that had taken me from Indiana to Australia had landed. International airports are sometimes treated as the most placeless of places, made up as they all are of so many seemingly interchangeable parts, from branches of the Body Shop, to shelves stocked everywhere with some of the same duty free goods, to bars dispensing identical drinks in Seattle, Seoul, and Stockholm. And yet, give any airport even "a bit of scrutiny," and you soon notice that distinctive things set each apart from all of its supposed doppelgangers. Give any one a "bit of thought" and just how distinctive it is begins to be clear. Where but the Detroit airport would a gift shop sell "Motownopoly," a customized version of the classic board game that has R&B songs as the key "properties" for sale? Where but SFO, near Napa, would there be wine tasting? Where but LAX would there be "Encounter," a restaurant that looks like its interior came straight out of a Jetsons cartoon and is described on its website as a place with "135-foot high parabolic arches and a futuristic design" and a "space-age interior," and was the location of one of the dinners for the Urban Icons conference? Where but Chicago's Midway Airport would there be giant statues of the Blues Brothers, fictional local heroes (or anti-heroes) played on screen by John Belushi and Dan Aykroyd? And where but Sydney would the most eye-catching sight you see when waiting to collect your baggage be statues of athletes, whose torsos seem to be emerging organically from the poles that hold up the ceiling?

It did not take any complex act of interpretation to figure out why, if there were to be sculptures in a baggage claim area, the ones in Sydney should be of individual men and women engaged in athletic acts, such as the female swimmer whose outstretched arms jutted out over the United Airlines carousel where I stood waiting for my suitcase. Clearly these were either left-over from or intentional reminders of the 2000 Olympics—the first of several things I encountered during my stay that made it clear that at least some within the city are eager to keep that event alive in the minds of visitors.* These remnants or reminders of the Olympics set me wondering whether other cities also have particular events in their past that are similarly identified with a moment of special global prominence. And I also began to muse on whether there were specific sites as well as specific moments in each of the world's major cities that stand out as speaking to their engagement with far-flung places or global aspirations, either in the present or in the past.

I mention this game last, even though it was inspired by something I saw during my first moments in Sydney, because the notion of trying to figure out, during a visit, what some of the key global moments or most worldly places in a city did not come to mind until after I had left Australia. This fits with Stilgoe's claim that one pay-off of "exploring" is that new thoughts about things you have encountered continue to form long after you have left the place

---

* The most amusing thing of this sort I saw was on the website of the University of New South Wales: a headline stating "UNSW hosts history Olympics," showing that, much to my surprise, what I had thought of as my own private nickname for the meetings was being used as a very public shorthand for them. I later learned, from a colleague who formerly taught at UNSW, that such nomenclature would come naturally at that institution, which has a "Centre for Olympic Studies" that holds workshops and sponsors publications relating to everything from the history and politics of the Games to their impact on traffic flows in host cities.

A life-size statue of John Belushi in one of his most famous roles at a Blues Brothers shop in Chicago's Midway Airport. *Photograph by Alan Thomas, used by permission.*

where you saw them. One way they come is via mentally revisiting sights and sounds and even smells of a trip that has ended. This is what happened with me, only with a high-tech twist: it was during the long flight home, as I looked through the digital photographs I had taken, that it struck me that the swimmer's body emerging from the baggage carousel pillar was the very first sight I had seen in Australia. I have since played the game in real-time in several cities I have visited, including Boston and Taipei.

It is the kind of game, though, that can also be played out of time or retrospectively, simply by looking back at places you have been and asking questions such as the following: What part of that city was especially linked to global flows of people (as Ellis Island is in New York), objects (the way the British Museum is in London), or fashions (as department stores are in Hong Kong—and, of course, many other places)? Was there a particular moment in the past of that locale when pieces of the world came together there in a special way, as they did, say, in Chicago during the 1893 Columbian Exposition or Tokyo in the year of its first Olympic Games? And are there particular parts of a metropolis that seem to serve as a magnet for visitors from far-flung destinations? Particularly interesting is to look for strong traces of the global showing up in unexpected places or less obvious moments, or if showing up in expected locales (museums, malls, and so on) and periods (when a World's Fair or international sporting event was held, for example), doing so in a distinctive rather than generic manner (as was the case with the Sydney baggage carousel—as, after all, I have never seen anything comparable in the airports of other cities that once hosted the Olympics). As with all the games I have described in this chapter, the biggest pay-off comes from the element of surprise, finding juxtapositions that were not quite what you thought you would find. The explorer, as Stilgoe might have put it, though this line is not in his book, treasures moments of discovery, even if all that is discovered is a small variation to a general pattern.

So, then, where besides the Sydney airport have I found surprising traces of the global? One place was in the greater Boston area, the first American metropolitan district I visited after thinking up this game. I didn't think I would have a chance to play the game properly, as I was in town to attend an old friend's wedding, which was to take place in Cambridge, and I was determined to spend the little extra time I had scheduled into my visit, besides the service and associated festivities, doing only two things. One was poking around in the stacks of Harvard's Yenching (East Asian materials) and Widener (general research collection) libraries. The other was catching up on the personal lives and academic projects of a few friends in the area whose research interests overlap with mine. If I had more time, I thought, it would be interesting to look around downtown Boston and see what I could discover about the city's links to and view of its place in the world. But that would just have to wait for another visit.

Soon after this thought had formed in my mind, though, I realized that Harvard Yard was about as worldly a place as there was in the greater Boston area—and not just for the obvious reasons, such as that students from many countries come there to study, libraries such as Widener contain books from or at least about every continent, and the university has museums as well that contain objects from disparate places. No, there was more to Harvard's global nature than that, and something to suggest that the dawn of the twenty-first century is a particularly global moment for this venerable institution: the presence of international tour groups. I spent two years studying at Harvard in the early 1980s, and I have no memory of seeing groups of this sort during the many times I crossed the Yard. There might, of course, have been occasional ones then, but had there been as many as I saw in 2005, I would surely have remembered.

It is not that strange that Harvard should have made its way onto tourist itineraries, but the fact that the Yard seemed filled that day with clusters of travelers speaking Japanese, Chinese, and German was striking. And when I mentioned what I had noticed (and sketched out this "Global Moments and Worldly Places" game idea) to two Harvard-based ethnographer friends, they assured me that the campus had become a very important tourist destination indeed. They also noted that the tour groups tended to follow ritualized procedures, making their way to particular buildings, stopping by certain statues, hearing guides tell standard bits of local folklore, and ending up at the same sacred site: a store selling Harvard sweatshirts and t-shirts to be taken home to prove that they had completed the pilgrimage. When I went to the store on Harvard Square my friends pointed me to, I found that its doorway was indeed as "global" a spot as one could hope to find, so varied were the languages being spoken by those entering it in search of and exiting it clasping pieces of crimson clothing.

Why has Harvard become such a must-see sight for international tourists? If this is a "global moment" for the school, what explains the timing? Is it a matter of age, that Harvard now seems old enough to attain the same footing as, say, the Oxbridge colleges? Or a matter of empire, which makes Harvard seem linked to global power in the way that those schools once did (though recent U.S. presidents have more often had links to Yale, a school that is less of a tourist draw)? I don't have a good answer. For Chinese tourists, though, the Harvard brand name has the advantage of being linked to a recent runaway best-seller and publishing phenomenon: *Harvard Girl Yiting Liu,* which purports to detail the "scientifically proven methods" that two parents used to help their daughter not only get into but also receive a full scholarship from the American university.

What then of Taipei? Two locations stand out as of particular interest, albeit for different reasons. One is the Chiang Kai-shek Memorial, the other the bamboo-shaped skyscraper known as Taipei 101.

With the memorial, what one finds is not so much a natural coming together of international elements as a forced effort to gloss over the degree to which Taiwan in Chiang Kai-shek's day and after has tended to be made peripheral to certain kind of global flows—marked by such things as the PRC bumping it out of bodies such as the UN. To encourage visitors to forget this marginalization, the memorial contains various displays that flag far-flung international connections. During my 2005 visit, for example, one of the most eye-catching sights was a pair of black 1950s vintage luxury cars, described as one-time possessions of the Generalissimo that had been purchased and donated by Chinese emigrés to the Philippines. And in a nearby exhibit hall, the walls were covered with photographs showing the Generalissimo and his charismatic wife, Soong Mei-ling (one of the Soong Sisters of Emily Hahn's famous book by that name), in the company of American presidents (Lyndon Johnson, Ronald Reagan, and others) and other top foreign dignitaries. One thing that I might have missed, if the American historian accompanying me on my tour of the site hadn't point it out, was something that was revealed by a close look at the dates of the photographs. Many of them were taken either before or after the foreign politician's period of greatest power, since for sitting American presidents and their counterparts in many other countries to go to Taipei has often been impossible, unless they were willing to risk greatly straining relations with Beijing.

The global dimensions of Taiwan's best-known skyscraper are more readily apparent, and they have been flagged continually in public statements by local officials such as Ma Ying-jeou, who was the mayor of the capital when Taipei 101 was built. According to an October 17, 2003, report by the Reuters news service, the following was Ma's most quotable line at the ceremony that accompanied the addition of the spire that made the skyscraper taller (at 1,667 feet) than the Petronas Towers in Malaysia (previous holders of the world's tallest building title): "I have no doubt that [this structure] can bring Taipei to the world and bring the world to Taipei." And throughout Taipei 101, there are images, objects, stores, and restaurants that reinforce this idea—especially the bringing "the world to Taipei" part of it. The first several floors of the building, for example, are given over to a high-ceilinged multi-level mall filled with stores selling an international array of luxury goods (jewelry, fashionable clothing, and so forth) and more ordinary objects (including a very impressive array of English language titles at a branch of the Singapore-based Page One bookstore). There are also restaurants that showcase tastes from a dozen or so cuisines (including several Chinese regional ones) and the bags and leaflets emblazoned with the global iconic line-ups mentioned earlier.

Most intriguingly of all, though, is a design feature that is built into the floor of the fourth level, and can be appreciated either by walking on top of it or gazing down upon it from above. It is a large circle made up of pieces of polished black stone, with the names of different cities and countries written on them. The selection of place names seems random, neither alphabetical nor geographical in orientation. Yet this seems fitting, in a sense, for the kind of global hodge-podge often found in contemporary malls, such as that which makes up the lowest levels of Taipei 101.

Go without a purpose.
Go for the going.

—John R. Stilgoe, *Outside Lies Magic*

The games described here were developed to help pass the time in places I had to go to for other reasons, and some of them have an implied agenda. This makes them very different exploratory exercises than those Stilgoe had in mind. In a sense, though, the games sketched out above can help inspire just the sort of going "without a purpose" that he encourages in his book. Curiosity about where representations of urban icons will show up on store shelves and on the streets of a city (in Shanghai, for instance, both the Customs House and Pearl of the Orient Tower appear in ads for alcoholic drinks and on city beautification posters) can make it more tempting than it already would have been to spend jet-lagged dawns wandering the streets of a foreign metropolis without any intended destination. So, too, can an interest in finding unfamiliar things that can be put to the "trend or dead-end" test.

Stilgoe insists that one can learn important lessons (especially about the past, but also sometimes about the present) from the kind of examination of everyday spaces he calls for, so one question that the reader might ask is whether I think there are things to be learned, rather than just diversion to be gained, from the games that I have been describing. I think so, though perhaps these are not so much lessons as suggestions for things worthy of more consideration than they sometimes get in popular discussions of globalization. One issue, for example, that all of the games encourage us to ponder is the phenomenon that geographer David Harvey has drawn attention to in one of the essays in his *Spaces of Capital:* namely, capitalism in its present stage both pushes major cities to become more like one another (in part so that an international managerial class can

Inside Taipei 101. A seemingly random selection of global place names are written on the band of black stone that encircles tables at the left side of the image. *Photograph by the author.*

feel comfortable and have access to similar services in all of them) and to remain distinctive (in part simply so tourists, who are part of what is now a giant industry, will continue to think it worth going from place to place). It could be that the importance of urban icons, both within and beyond the cities they represent, is becoming more and more significant, since their use can be part of a strategy for ac-centuating a sense of the specialness of a place and counteracting any fear that homogenizing forces have gone too far. To put this an-other way, if the time comes when there is a Starbucks in every city (there were not yet any in Finland as of January of 2006, but there was a Subway franchise near my hotel in Turku), reminders that only some of them are within walking distance of the Shanghai Cus-toms House, Taipei 101, or the Opera House may seem all the more necessary.

A more general lesson or thing to ponder suggested by all of these games is that to understand the curious interplay of old and new and domestic and international in contemporary times, and to make sense of the many forms that hybridity can take, as people and fash-ions and objects jostle and collide and are combined in new ways in different locales, you still have to go places and look around. Curi-ously, this is also one of the lessons I took away from Thomas Fried-man's *The World Is Flat,* which seems at first glance a work that ar-gues for the rapidly diminishing importance of place and the local. His is a breathless account of the way that—due to the capability of new, ever-faster, and further-reaching technologies of communica-tion and transportation to link disparate locales—everything is be-coming something that, at least potentially, can be outsourced, made, or in the case of services delivered, any there instead of any here.

Friedman gives many examples of experiences or discoveries that led him to a new appreciation of how the world is being "flattened," which in his use of the term means becoming a place across which people, things, and ideas can travel with a minimum of friction (of the sort caused by physical or political barriers). One particularly in-triguing example is his account of the time he spent in Bangalore, India, during a visit that included seeing the video conferencing fa-cility that allowed a local entrepreneur to conduct real-time meet-ings with colleagues scattered around the globe, during which he could not just hear what others were saying but also watch their facial expressions. The vignette, like so many of Friedman's, is striking and reported well, even if, as in other cases, he might have been well served by asking some version of the "trend or dead-end" question.

What is interesting to me upon reflection, though, is that the overall impression I was left with of his trip to Bangalore was that what he found there was a place that was not like any other (suggesting place still matters) and that his analysis of global trends will no longer be worth reading if he ever stops going abroad (as outside of our ordinary paths lies not just magic but clues to a confusing global present).

16. Faster than a Speeding Bullet Train

Throughout the ride to the hotel, the streets along the way [in San Francisco] were large and grand, and the houses and buildings towering and lofty—more so than in Shanghai.
　　　　—Li Gui, *A New Account of a Trip Around the Globe,* 1878

Shanghai is mad for skyscrapers—it has more than the entire West Coast of the US. . . .
　　　　—*The Guardian,* November 8, 2004

Shanghai is no stranger to superlatives, and in the September 27, 2004, issue of its Asian edition, *Time Magazine* added a new one to the list: the phrase "world's most happening city" was used to accompany a brightly hued image of the metropolis that graced the periodical's front cover. Prior to that, at one time or another, Shanghai had been called the "most cosmopolitan," "most decadent," "most dynamic," and "most exciting" city on earth, as well as the richest, hippest, and biggest and most fashionable, most sinful, and most sophisticated urban center in China. It has also long been (and still is) routinely described as the Chinese city that seems "most modern," thanks in part to it having so many tall buildings. One gets a sense of just how long this idea has been in place from the comment above by Li Gui, the Chinese world traveler. When Li set off to circle the globe (on his 1876 trip that included a long stopover at the Philadelphia World's Fair), Shanghai was not yet home to the riverfront neo-classical and art deco riverfront buildings still featured on postcards. Most of these (the domed Hong Kong and Shanghai Bank, the clock-towered Customs House, the green-roofed Cathay Hotel) date from the 1920s and 1930s. Nevertheless, Li still found it natural in the account of his trip first published in 1878 to use the shorter Shanghai landmarks of his day as benchmarks against which to measure the "loftiness" of foreign edifices.

As colorful as *Time*'s recent addition to the long list of superlatives given to this "most modern" metropolis in China was, a still more interesting one was provided a few months previously by Giorgio Armani, who may be no expert on urbanization but definitely knows a thing or two about trends. He was quoted in the April 19, 2004, issue of the *China Daily* as having told a reporter in Beijing: "Today's Shanghai certainly qualifies as the most talked about city in the world." Why was Shanghai on the designer's mind? Because he was heading there to help launch a glitzy new Armani Store located on the ground floor of Three on the Bund, a refurbished riverfront landmark that is now topped by an open-air restaurant that affords diners a view of some of the most famous icons of old and new Shanghai, from the Customs House and Peace Hotel down the street to the exponentially taller 88-story Jinmao Tower across the river in Pudong, which is now the tallest skyscraper in China.

Armani's claim, like *Time*'s, is hard to prove, but the shape-shifting metropolis that now has a foot placed firmly on each side of the Huangpu River is definitely generating an enormous amount of talk—and writing. And this makes it interesting to ask how the things being said about it locally and globally now compare to things that were said about it in earlier periods. The 1930s, for example, when *Fortune* magazine ran its first color spread on the city, presenting it as an anything-goes boomtown whose skyline had recently undergone a dramatic change. It was also in 1930s that Ni Yiying insisted, in a wonderfully detailed Chinese language guide to the city called simply *Shanghai*, that some of his countrymen might not be able to tell you what the nation's capital was called—and yet

The clock tower to the left, which is now dwarfed by the skyscraper to its right, belonged to what was once the Racing Club of Shanghai's International Settlement, then later became a public library, and now serves as an art museum. At the time it was built, late in the city's treaty-port century (1843–1943), it was one of Shanghai's tallest and most modern-looking structures. *Photograph by the author.*

even they were familiar with the famed place name "Shanghai," associating it with the very latest products, ideas, and fashions.

There are definitely many echoes of 1930s commentaries to be heard in the current global chatter on Shanghai, as even these brief comments suggest. (And as for occasional complaints that upon arrival, today's Shanghai fails to live up to all the hype—well, those too have 1930s precursors.) So much seems familiar at first, in fact, that (though ultimately misleading) it is tempting to build on the cinematic metaphor of Akbar Abbas (who describes Shanghai's rapidly changing built environment as a case of the "city as remake, a shot-by-shot reworking of a classic") and think of the current "talk" as an adaptation of a familiar film script that has stayed close to the original source. It is impossible, of course, to ignore one big contrast with the 1930s: Shanghai is no longer a quasi-colonial treaty port broken up into Chinese-run and foreign-run districts. But the temptation that needs to be avoided is to assume that, leaving aside contrasts associated with the disappearance of a system of foreign privilege, the current discourse on the city is the rhetorical equivalent to the material phenomenon that cultural critic Abbas outlines in his fascinating essay "Play It Again Shanghai: Urban Preservation in the Global Era."

Following in the footsteps of Abbas is certainly seductive for two reasons. Cinematic metaphors seem custom-made for a city that has been featured in films by von Sternberg (*Shanghai Express* and *Shanghai Gesture*), Spielberg (*Empire of the Sun* and *Indiana Jones and the Temple of Doom*), Zhang Yimou (*Shanghai Triad*), and a Merchant-Ivory production (*The White Countess*). The other reason the idea is seductive is that, as in the 1930s, the city is once again being lauded with superlatives, compared to leading urban centers of the West, and described as the site of unusual juxtapositions.

In the end, however, it just won't do to think of the current discourse on Shanghai as merely a straightforward reworking of a familiar script that has been updated for an era of Chinese control of the city. One problem with this notion is that there are significant new twists even to what seem at first simply to be restated old superlatives. 1930s references to Shanghai containing the tallest building *in Asia* or seeming the fastest-paced city *in China,* for example, are quite different from recent statements that in a few years Pudong will be home to the tallest building *in the world* and that the metropolis by the Huangpu seems now to be moving at a quicker rate than any other place *on earth*. And an even more interesting case of unpacking an apparent continuity and discovering a dramatic rupture relates to the way New York–Shanghai comparisons typically worked seventy years ago and the way they often work today.

Treaty port–era Shanghai was routinely called the "Paris of the East," but it was also often described as China's counterpart to New York. And when this was done, particularly in Western texts, the tendency was to present Shanghai as characterized by a peculiar mixture of elements: it had signature buildings reminiscent of Manhattan yet also rickshaws and opium dens. Bringing the vehicle and the drug into the picture marked Shanghai as exotic and underscored that, despite the impressive bank headquarters lining the Bund (called "China's Wall Street") and the department stores nearby on Nanjing Road (the "5th Avenue of the East"), it was still a metropolis straining to catch up with, not quite one in the same league as, New York. Now, once again, the city is often said to resemble New York, but with some differences. Moreover, sometimes an unusual mode of transportation, a drug, or both is mentioned to symbolize those differences. So far, so good, for those drawn to the "city as remake" idea.

Yet look at the rhetoric more carefully and some key distinctions emerge, beginning with the mode of transportation brought in to flag difference. It is now not the presence of rickshaws but of the rocket-like maglev train that is cited most often as something that helps set Shanghai off from New York. It is hard to think of a more striking contrast than that between these two vehicles, whether one has in mind sheer speed or symbolism. A rickshaw is slow, earthbound, and powered by a human being who has been reduced to animal-like status, while the maglev is rapidly propelled through space by unseen forces, reaching speeds that exceed by quite a bit those of even France's TGV and Japan's famed Bullet Train.

Changes relating to drug references tell a similar tale, with soporific opium mentioned less often now than synthetic compounds associated with such things as rapid heart rates, flurries of activity, and artificially enhanced strength. The worry over local actual usage of ecstasy and ice (a form of speed) is matched in the realm of symbolism by descriptions of Shanghai as having become a "city on steroids" (*Condé Nast Traveler,* May 2001, and *New York Times,* November 28, 2004); Pudong looking like "Manhattan on acid" (*International Herald Tribune,* May 18, 2004); and local skyscrapers resembling Western ones put "on amphetamines" (*International Herald Tribune,* November 19, 2002). The phrase "New York on steroids" has even been used to refer to the skyline (*Print Week,* November 11, 2004) and city as a whole (*National Post* [Canada], July 17, 2004, and *USA Today,* October 28, 2004). This phrase combines awe at speedy development with concern about excess, suggesting Shanghai might end up surpassing former rivals in the short term, but at the cost of endangering its long-term well being, in the same way that athletes do by taking performance-enhancing drugs.

In Shanghai itself there has also been an explosion of commentary about local developments (bookstores now routinely devote considerable numbers of shelves and much display space to photographic histories, guidebooks, and publications that ruminate on where the metropolis has been, is now, and might be heading), and the possible dangers of excess are discussed in some of these. But while optimism and pessimism jockey for supremacy in foreign reports, the former carries the day in most publications produced near the Huangpu, which tend to assert that the city will manage to pull off the trick of combining breakneck growth with long-term safety. To put this another way, the local and global discourses converge tightly around one notion (Shanghai is definitely futuristic) while diverging at times on another (how much bursting forward into the future is likely to cost the metropolis and its residents, including migrant construction workers who can't afford to buy a cappuccino at one of the many new branches of Starbucks let alone anything on display at Three on the Bund, and the hundreds of thousands of denizens of central districts scheduled to be relocated to outlying areas in the next decade or so to ease the strain on the infrastructure of the city center).

Though different answers may be given, the following questions (which certainly deserve to be asked) are often being posed both inside and outside of Shanghai. Are enough older buildings being protected, enough new parks being built, and enough effort being made to keep the chasm between rich and poor from growing still larger and perhaps leading to outbursts of social unrest? And is enough care being taken to ensure that the 2010 World Expo, which could bring as many as 70 million tourists to the city, will not prove too much for the local transportation network to handle?

It is interesting to note that one point on which consensus seems to have emerged both globally and locally is that Shanghai is now an eminently logical place to hold the aforementioned World Expo. This is noteworthy because that event is intended to carry forward the World's Fair tradition—dating back to the Philadelphia Centennial Exposition that Li Gui attended, and indeed still further to the Crystal Palace Exhibition of 1851—of showcasing not only international diversity but also new inventions and state of the art technologies that give visitors a taste of what the future will be like. In 1876, to see either the world or the future on display, Li Gui had to travel from Shanghai to the other side of the globe. By the 1930s, Shanghai would have seemed to provide an ideal site for an event devoted to one half of that World's Fair mission, the international one, since it contained within its borders representatives of more than fifty nationalities. But it would have still been hard then to make a case for it as a logical place to put the future on display. It was thought of as unusually modern *for a city located in China,* but hardly futuristic. Or, rather, only futuristic to someone coming to it from a locale that lacked tall buildings, neon lights, elevators, trams, and other symbols of early-twentieth-century modernity.

This brings us to the biggest flaw in the "city as remake" approach, which has to do with a subtle but crucial shift in visions of Shanghai as a metropolis of curious juxtapositions: such juxtapositions now are often imagined to have more to do with temporalities than with cultures. Shanghai is still seen as a place made special in part by the coming together of Chinese and foreign elements, but increasingly even more focus is put on the co-existence within a single city of evocations of many different eras, ranging from the pre-treaty-port past to the future.

One genre of foreign text that has registered this shift very clearly is the guidebook. In these, emphasis on Shanghai as a metropolis of varied temporalities as well as a meeting point of cultures has grown markedly in the last two decades. To flag this, many feature on their covers images linked to different periods. And the focus on the city as palimpsest is continued inside. Consider, for example, the 2004 edition of the Lonely Planet's *Shanghai City Guide*. Upon opening this book, the first thing readers find, opposite the table of contents page, is a set of five photographs that go with a list of "The Top Five" Shanghai sights. Number 1 is a shot of the Bund, with the Customs House looming large close to the viewer and the art deco Peace Hotel fading out near the edge of the frame. The caption linked to this photograph reads: "Walk Shanghai's most impressive mile, where old meets new" (note: not where "East meets West," as older guide books often put it). Number 2 is a shot of the Jinmao Tower, photographed looking a bit like a rocket about to take off for outer space. Number 3 is a shot of balconies in the former French Concession, described as an example of the "1930s architecture" ready to be discovered by those who explore the backstreets. Number 4 is a shot of porcelain figurines striking revolutionary poses, presented as examples of the sort of "Mao memorabilia" for sale in antique stalls. And Number 5 is a shot of the new Shanghai Museum, touted as the best in the country and a place where "4,000 years of culture" is on display to all who enter. The back cover of the book invites readers to "WALK THROUGH TIME," via routes that take them through "the Bund, the French Concession, and the Old Town" (that last section described elsewhere as a district that long predates the treaty-port era).

Not all of these eras are emphasized in texts produced in Shanghai: for example, locally produced guidebooks are less likely to point people toward places to buy Maoist kitsch. Still, in local publications, too, there is increasing focus on the juxtaposition of periods and attention paid to nostalgia, particularly for the fabled 1930s. There are many coffee table books devoted exclusively to then-and-now photographs (black-and-white for the old, color for the new) of particular parts of the city. There have also been books produced that combine images of the past and present with images of future projects still in the design phase—though the most visually stunning foray into this genre, Seng Kuan and Peter G. Rowe's *Shanghai: Ar-*

chitecture & Urbanism for Modern China, was published in Germany, albeit with a multinational contributors' list that includes PRC-based urban planner Wu Yue, leading French Sinologist Marie-Claire Bergère, and influential Chicago-based theorist of globalization Saskia Sassen.

In addition to publications, the new focus on juxtaposed eras shows through in the built form and slogans associated with some tourist attractions. An influential case in point is the newly built but old-looking Xintiandi entertainment district. This is filled with structures self-consciously designed to remind visitors of the look of Shanghai buildings of the early 1900s. (Built in the Shikumen style, a hybrid form made up of Chinese and Western elements, some of these structures even contain material saved from old buildings in the area that were torn down to make room for the development.) Meanwhile, food and drink choices are emphatically contemporary: visitors can sample fusion cuisine, linger over a latte, or drink rum at "Che's," a bar that promiscuously combines evocations of revolutionary Cuba and decadent Old Havana. The district's motto: "Where yesterday meets tomorrow in the Shanghai of Today."

Another place where yesterday and tomorrow come together in curious ways is the Urban Planning Museum, a site that has bequeathed to Shanghai yet another superlative, containing as it does the world's largest scale model of a city. When approaching the main entrance, one sees, before going inside, a large countdown clock that ticks off the days left until Shanghai takes the global center stage as host of the World Expo. Then, immediately upon entering, one thing visitors see is a giant gold-colored revolving statue, which includes stylized replicas of 1920s and 1930s landmarks of the Bund, towered over by both extant Pudong skyscrapers and the (as of early 2007) still-to-be-completed World Financial Center, which upon completion will soar higher than Taipei 101 and is slated to become, for a time, the tallest building on earth. Visitors can then go up and get a view of the scale model of the city, which is not how it is but how it is expected to be soon, when the Expo will be in town, the World Financial Center will have been completed, and the world's largest Ferris Wheel (slated to be 35 meters taller than the London Eye, according to some reports) will stand by the Huangpu. To make sure that visitors do not forget the past while thinking of the future, though, other sights on the upper floors include sepia photos of old Shanghai and a walk-through exhibit on Chinese participation in past World's Fairs.

Another sort of reminder of the past can be found beneath the entry level: a series of storefronts and wax figures designed to replicate Shanghai circa 1930—one of many such replicas scattered throughout the city, the most elaborate of which are part of the Shanghai History Museum housed in basement of the Pearl of the Orient Tower. Finally, visitors can buy either forward-looking or backward-looking objects inside the museum, including then-and-now photography books of the sort mentioned above. And, at least during my 2002 stop at the museum, they could buy *Zoujin shibo-hui* (Entering the World Expo), a small illustrated book filled with images of old World's Fairs and excited references to the bid Shanghai had then recently launched to host a future one. One thing that makes that book memorable to me is that it was while reading it that I first came across Li Gui's name and a short description of his 1876 world tour.

Having come back to this Phileas Fogg–like figure, it seems fitting to end this chapter that has dealt in part with visions of the future with some comments on Jules Verne, a writer associated at least as much with futurology as with travel. In *Around the World in Eighty Days*, Fogg never quite makes it to Shanghai, though he is en route there at one point, before getting diverted to Japan. A few years later, however, Verne made up for this by having Kin-Fo, the protagonist of another book (admittedly a much less well-known one), *Les Tribulations d'un Chinois en Chine* (1879), be a resident of Shanghai. One thing that intrigues me about this is that Verne describes Kin-Fo as a "progressive man, who was not opposed to the importation of each and every modern invention," something that differentiated him sharply, according to the author, from those more reactionary Chinese, such as "behind-the-times mandarins," who objected to such things as telegraph wires being run over land and cables being laid under the sea. Kin-Fo is even described as having "lighted his house with gas" and "adopted phonography," a means

2010 World Expo Countdown Clock located outside of Shanghai's Urban Planning Museum. *Photograph by the author.*

of communication that had recently been "brought to the highest degree of perfection by Edison."

What all this indicates is that, as early as 1879 (the same year that General Grant made a stop in the treaty port), Shanghai was both famous enough in the West to attract Verne's attention, and was the sort of place thought of as a natural one in which to find those Chinese who were most interested in keeping up with the latest trends. It is important to note, though, that this is one of the books by Verne that lacks anything futuristic, as opposed to just things that are up-to-date for the author's own times. Shanghai, this suggests, seemed at best the kind of place where someone might stay abreast of developments, but hardly a place to look to for breakthroughs.

Shanghai would begin to inspire futuristic fantasies by Chinese writers around the start of the twentieth century (including a fragment of a science fiction novel by the famous literary and political figure Liang Qichao that described a great international exhibition taking place by the Huangpu in the far-off year of 1962), but it is only very recently that foreign observers have begun to break with Verne and treat the metropolis as capable of setting as opposed to merely following trends. Philip Dodd probably overstated the case a bit when, writing in *The Guardian* (July 30, 2004), he claimed: "Ask anyone what city in the world feels like the future and they will nominate Shanghai." But there is something to what he says.

A variety of works could be cited to illustrate Shanghai's growing reputation as a city that seems to anticipate an urban future that could be wonderful, horrific, or combine appealing and appalling features. A list of these would include everything from Neal Stephenson's *The Diamond Age*, a 1995 Hugo Award–winning cyberpunk novel set in a Shanghai of the future, to *Have You Been Shanghaied?*, a short bilingual book by Singapore-based architect and urban theorist William Lim, who is optimistic about where the city is heading.

Perhaps the best illustration, though, of just how far things have come relates to how this enduringly cinematic metropolis is now being used in films. Merchant-Ivory decided to shoot there for a familiar reason: old landmark buildings continue to exist that can be integrated easily into a tale set during the city's legendary treaty-port era (though not quite as easily as when Spielberg made *Empire of the Sun* there in 1987, since more care must be taken now to keep the edge of the frame from including an anarchronistic image, such as a satellite dish or new skyscraper). But what brought Tom Cruise to Shanghai during the making of *Mission Impossible III*, a 2006 release, was something different—a decision by the film's creators that Pudong had the look of a fast-paced twenty-first-century city. Nor is it why director Michael Winterbottom shot scenes for his first science fiction film, *Code 46*, a 2004 release, in new landmark buildings such as the Jinmao Tower across the river from the Peace Hotel (a setting used in *The White Countess*). Winterbottom was drawn to Pudong because he thought that audiences would think its skyscrapers ("loftier" than anything Li Gui or, for that matter, Jules Verne ever saw) were far less likely to belong to the world of today than to the world of tomorrow.

Afterword: Rhymes for Our Times

The name of Marco Polo is scratched onto the minds of almost every American schoolchild [conjuring up] powerful images of China's ancient greatness. . . . [We also associate the Chinese with a] heavy cluster of admirable qualities [that are] identified in our own generation with the people of Pearl Buck novels, solid, simple, courageous folk. . . .

Genghiz Khan and his Mongol hordes are the non-Chinese ancestors of quite another set of images also strongly associated with the Chinese: cruelty, barbarism, inhumanity. . . .

In the long history of our associations with China, these two sets of images rise and fall, move in and out of the center of people's minds, never wholly displacing each other. . . .

—Harold Isaacs, *Scratches on Our Minds,* 1958

History does not repeat itself, but it does rhyme.
—Bruce Sterling, "Viridian Design," from a speech given
October 14, 1998

"There's nothing new under the sun." "History repeats itself." These kinds of sayings have always bothered me, despite or maybe because I teach and write about the past for a living. The phrases bother me even though when I contribute articles to newspapers or magazines or give classroom lectures or talks to general audiences, I often argue that soundbite-driven forms of mass media pay too little attention to the historical roots of contemporary dilemmas. The phrases bother me even though, in those settings and when writing things such as textbook chapters, I often insist that issues associated with China or globalization or protest are best understood when placed in long-term historical perspective. And the phrases bother me even though I am very fond of using analogies drawn from the past to think about the present. The phrases bother me, despite all this, because looking backward in a manner that is sensitive to both continuities and ruptures is very different from falling into the trap of assuming that we have been in a situation exactly like the current one before, or the trap of thinking of history as always staying within pre-set grooves.

I am probably particularly sensitive to the damage done by visions of history as repetitious because of how strong the tendency has been for Westerners, and sometimes Chinese commentators as well, to treat China as strangely impervious to change or able at best to move in a cyclical fashion. Navigating between the Scylla of ignoring the past and the Charybdis of viewing history as a strait jacket that constricts Chinese possibilities often proves tricky, as I have discovered over and over again in relation to the upheavals of 1989. Not surprisingly, given that I finished a dissertation on pre-1949 student protests a month before the hunger strikes began at Tiananmen Square and two months before the June 4th Massacre, throughout the last decade of the twentieth century I devoted a great deal of attention to China's 1989. And I often insisted that the events of that year could best be understood (indeed could only be fully understood) by taking into account the degree to which they were influenced by, and at times paralleled in specific ways, pre-1949 protests, some of which had been fueled by similar grievances (anger at corruption, for example) and been brutally suppressed. Still, while taking issue with present-minded understandings of Tiananmen (that tended to overstate both the parallels with the nearly contemporaneous upheavals in Eastern Europe and the influence of American ideas on Beijing protesters), I was concerned from the start with analytical moves that used this Chinese upheaval to breathe new life into the old canard of a "changeless" China. As deeply critical as I was (and remain) of the brutal steps that the regime took to crush the protests, it was troubling to see complex developments fit neatly into very old frameworks. It disturbed me, for example, that one of the English language books on the PRC that made the biggest splash early in the 1990s was Harrison Salisbury's *The New Emperors: China in the Era of Mao and Deng.*

It is certainly true that many countries, including China, have experienced revolutions that were supposed to change everything, yet still ended up with new orders that shared important characteristics with the *ancien régimes* that revolutionaries had been determined to displace. (This is a danger that, in their own distinctive ways, both Tocqueville and Marx warned of in their writings.) And it is also true that in China's case (again, not uniquely), a tendency to treat challengers to the authority of the state in a harsh manner has been one of the worst things to be carried over from the *ancien régime* into the revolutionary new order—a point 1989 underscored. Still, to note continuities is one thing, but it is something else to let them lead one to lose sight of novelties, such as the many ways in which Mao and even more so Deng were different from emperors and governed a country that had been radically altered since imperial times.

The simple fact is that within the PRC, there have been and continue to be some genuinely new things going on under the sun. The Marriage Law of 1950, which treated men and women as free agents and equal partners in forming relationships, is a case in point. Whether or not its strictures were fully carried out, it represented a dramatic break with pre-revolutionary traditions. Or consider issues of succession. The very top leadership position in the PRC has not, as was often the case in China of the imperial era, been passed from father to son. More recently, the dramatic manner in which China has gone from being an overwhelmingly rural country to one in which nearly half of the people live in cities has been an unprecedented development, some of the implications of which will only become clear in the decades to come. And as the preceding chapter on Shanghai argued, even some new trends that seem at first to be replays of the past turn out, on closer scrutiny, to involve ruptures as well as links to earlier times.

Given my concern with the need to neither overstate nor understate the power of the past to shape the present, it was a godsend when a student brought my attention to Bruce Sterling's "Veridian Design" speech, which the science fiction writer delivered at the Yerba Buena Center for the Arts in San Francisco and then posted on the web (prefaced by the following statement in red: "Ideological Freeware—Distribute at Will").* Devoted in part to arguing that there were intriguing parallels between the 1890s and the 1990s, relating to everything from technological breakthroughs in the realm of communication to patterns of global instability, Sterling's presentation may not have been the first to refer to history's tendency to "rhyme" rather than repeat itself. (There is, in fact, as a bit of googling reveals, an ongoing debate on the web over whether the phrase Sterling uses or one very like it was originally coined by Mark Twain, or whether attributing it to Samuel Clemens is just one more in a long line of fallacious attributions of this sort.) It was, though, a new phrase to me when it was brought to my attention, and it immediately struck me as something that I wished I had been familiar with earlier, as it could have helped me, for example, clarify my view of China's 1989 when I had tried to write about Tiananmen at moments such as the tenth anniversary of the June 4th Massacre in 1999.

How would Sterling's phrase have aided me in writing about Tiananmen? I might well have argued that, when it came to grievances and tactics, while the protests of 1989 did not exactly parallel any previous Chinese ones, they did "rhyme" with those of the Civil War era (1945–1949). During that period, students had also taken to the streets (and sometimes journeyed to the capital) to express their anger at the actions of a ruling party that they viewed as headed by corrupt individuals who were falling short of living up to the ideals of the Revolution, and in so doing endangering the well-being of the nation. The 1989 protests were hardly exact replays of events of that earlier period. Among the many differences: hunger strikes were a more important tactic in the Tiananmen protests than

---

* Last read on April 26, 2006, at http://www.viridiandesign.org/viridiandesign.htm.

in any Civil War protest, the capital city that students traveled to and in which they presented petitions of complaint in the 1940s was Nanjing as opposed to Beijing, and the organization in power then was the Nationalist Party rather than the CCP. In addition, there was no counterpart in 1989 to the underground members of the Communist Party, who often played key roles in mobilizing students to stage marches intended to shame the Nationalists. Still, words that rhyme are not the same, just have an important element in common, and this was true of the Civil War–era protests and those of 1989, though Americans who learned about Tiananmen from network newscasts would not have been aware of this.

Had I become acquainted with Sterling's speech right when it was given, I would also have been ready in 1999, when writing around the time of the tenth anniversary of the June 4th Massacre, to have presented the state violence of 1989 as having "rhymed" with several similar but not identical events. The May 30th Massacre of 1925, for instance, during which police in one of Shanghai's foreign-run districts fired into a crowd of unarmed protesters agitating against imperialism. Or the acts of state violence that created martyrs during Prague Spring—an Eastern European event that is in many regards a better match overall for China's 1989 than the contemporaneous Velvet Revolution, since many Tiananmen protesters, like their counterparts in the Soviet bloc in 1968, saw their goal as bringing about reform within—not the toppling of—the Communist Party.

Looking at the world of today and the issues raised throughout this book, armed with this new term for talking about parallels that are not sequels or remakes but something subtler, I can think of many different sorts of "rhymes" with the past worth noting. Some relate to global travel. It is very different to be able to cross an ocean in the span of hours via a jet rather than over the course of weeks in a steamship. And yet, as my earlier discussion of *Innocents Abroad* suggested, there are more than a few rhymes, or parallels with twists, linking past and present to be found when thinking about long-distance journeys.

Additional rhymes worth contemplating relate to other aspects of the globalization *avant la lettre* of the 1800s (the term only came into common use in the final decades of the 1900s) and the globalization proper of contemporary times. For example, there are moments when the optimistic reactions to increasingly rapid global flows of the Victorian era could easily be mistaken for a commentary on the present—and the same goes for pessimistic reactions to the speed with which the world seemed then and seems again now to be shrinking. Clear cases in point are provided by things written and said during the lead-up to the Crystal Palace Exhibition of 1851, the granddaddy of all World's Fairs. In an 1850 issue of the *Economist,* one of the few publications that has been around to cover global flows from Victorian times on up into the current still-young century, a speech by Prince Albert, a Crystal Palace booster, put the case for the optimists well—in a manner that rhymes with the rhetoric of optimists of the present. "Nobody," he claimed at one point, could doubt that they were living in "a period of wonderful transition" when "distances which separated the different nations" were "gradually vanishing" and "products of all quarters of the globe" were becoming readily available.

On the side of the pessimists, *Punch* ran a satiric piece in that same year, which took the form of a letter by a London mother worried by the new illnesses that might be brought to Britain by tourists pouring into the country to visit Crystal Palace. Titled "The Exhibition Plague," the text expresses concern about the damage that will be done when things such as the "black jaundice" (from America) and something called the "king's evil" (from Naples) reach London. These fears from the age of the telegraph and cholera epidemics rhyme with those of our age of the Internet and avian flu just as neatly as do Prince Albert's hopes.

A different set of rhymes that are easy to hear now relate to the American love-hate relationship with China that journalist Harold Isaacs described so well in his 1958 classic *Scratches on Our Minds.* There is, as Isaacs suggests, though never using this terminology of course, a recurrent rhyme scheme that can be detected in American thoughts and fantasies about China. Sometimes positive images of China (as a stable place of ageless wisdom) and the Chinese (as stolid figures who share our fundamental values) predominate. Sometimes negative images of China (as a chaotic place that threatens us) and the

Chinese (as members of a faceless horde) assume ascendancy (or, rather, resume it). Recurrence always comes with twists. That is, there are always specifics being added to and taken away from a common, though always growing, stock of images and there are different ways for elements of positive and negative fantasies to bleed into one another. Still, as Isaacs puts it, there are powerful recurrences, due to the enduring substrata of Pearl Buck and Fu Manchu dreams and nightmares that are "ready to emerge at the call of fresh circumstances, always new, yet instantly garbed in all the words and pictures of a much-written literature."

Thinking about specifics that give old visions new dimensions in current times, it makes a difference that now, as opposed to in the days of the Boxers, when Americans worry about a China threat, visions of a Chinese army that not only has an enormous population of potential recruits to draw upon but also high-tech weapons can be invoked. And it makes a difference that now, when Pearl Buck is again being read, more Americans than in the 1930s can conjure up the faces of Chinese celebrities linked to cosmopolitan and urban settings (basketball star Yao Ming, actresses such as Zhang Ziyi, and so on) and place them beside the *Good Earth*'s farming families in their minds. Nevertheless, specific alterations aside, there is much in American thinking about China that resonates with times past, despite the varied ways that the PRC has changed and continues to change.

As useful as Isaacs' framework remains, despite the passage of more than four decades since he carried out the interviews that served as the main basis for his study, it is worth remembering that American hopes and fears linked to the PRC sometimes rhyme with hopes and fears that in the past have been tied to other countries. Take, for example, the title that the *New York Review of Books* gave to an essay on the June 4th Massacre: "The Empire Strikes Back." This was an allusion to a *Star Wars* film, of course, and it might also have played upon the fact that China was once a land run by emperors that some Western commentators thought of as prone to behave as despots. But the phrase was also one that conjured up visions of a different sort, namely, of the PRC coming to replace the Soviet Union as the most threatening Communist country. After all,

Ronald Reagan had famously referred to Moscow as running an "Evil Empire" just a few years before Tiananmen.

Similarly, the demonic Chairman of Chang and Halliday's 2005 biography, *Mao: The Unknown Story,* rhymes with more than just Fu Manchu and the devilish Empress Dowager portrayed in the Boxer film *55 Days at Peking.* The figure they describe is one that resonates with and partly draws its power to terrify from the literature on totalitarian leaders of countries other than China, in particular Hitler. This is something that the authors of the book were clearly aware of when writing, since several times they invoke the name of that Nazi personification of evil, either to suggest that Mao was very like him or, in some cases, to suggest that Mao's record was in certain regards even worse.

A different sort of rhyming across national divides has to do with China and Japan, since there has often been a curious see-saw effect where American visions of these two countries are concerned: when one is up, the other is likely to be down. At the turn of the twentieth century, for example, Japan was celebrated for being a country that had discovered how to learn from and work with the West, and much was made of Japanese troops joining those of Western countries to suppress the Boxers. During World War II, China was up and Japan was down in the American imagination, and Hollywood churned out propaganda films that presented the Chinese as individuals who wanted the same things that their counterparts in the United States did, while the Japanese were represented as belonging to a faceless horde.

In the early part of the Cold War, this was all reversed. It was then the Chinese, not the Japanese, who were presented as part of an undifferentiated and potentially threatening crowd—an image put forth, for example, in a tellingly titled 1963 study of the PRC by George Paloczi-Horvath (that has much in common with Chang and Halliday's book), *Mao Tse-Tung: Emperor of the Blue Ants.* Another reversal took place a couple of decade ago, as fears of Japan's economic rise ran rampant. And it is that anti-Japanese discourse of the 1980s that seems to rhyme most purely with some of the contemporary commentaries on the economic threat to U.S. interests that China is posing or may soon pose. There is a familiar ring, for example, to the worries expressed in 2005 about Chinese interest in buying Western oil companies—familiar not because of previous worries expressed about China, but rather because of the kinds of things that were said in the 1980s about Japanese interest in buying up Los Angeles skyscrapers and New York City landmark buildings.

If we turn, finally, from American misunderstandings and simplifications of Chinese realities to China's current predicaments, what rhymes are there to listen for or hear mid-way through the first decade of the new millennium? Some of the most interesting resonances harken back, as the earlier reference to analogies between Tiananmen and the protests of the Civil War era suggested, to the last years of Chiang Kai-shek's rule of the mainland. Many problems and challenges faced by CCP leaders rhyme with those that ultimately forced the Nationalists to flee to Taiwan. Some of the strategies that the Beijing regime has pursued, such as jettisoning and modifying earlier revolutionary commitments to the point that it is hard to tell what their project stands for (other than a desire to make China strong through economic development while keeping it a single-party state), are ones that a Generalissimo brought back to life would recognize. And more than half a century before the CCP tried to leap ahead and steer patriotic outrage in loyalist directions, during the anti-NATO protests of 1999 and anti-Japanese ones of 2005, Chiang Kai-shek's regime had attempted in similar fashion to ride the tiger of popular nationalism.

Still, as illuminating as analogies to the Civil War era can be, it is crucial to think of China today as rhyming with as opposed to being just like what it once was. In part because otherwise it becomes too easy to assume that the Communists will soon suffer the same fate as the Nationalists, and it is by no means clear that they will. They might instead manage to stay in power but evolve into a radically different sort of organization—as some would argue has already occurred, since it has become an anomalous sort of Communist Party, to say the least, that accepts capitalists into its ranks. Certainly, at present, the prospects for an exact replay of 1949 are out of the question—there is no organized alternative party waiting in the wings as the Communists were when the Nationalists were defeated.

In addition, even when it comes to sources and patterns of discontent, while parallels with the past are important to note, there are novelties of the current moment that set it apart from the 1940s and even from the late 1980s. Some of the most significant protests early in this century have been of a hitherto unknown sort, in that they have been spurred by anger at the state failing to live up to what might be seen as a distinctively post-Tiananmen bargain with the people: allow us to retain a monopoly on political power, and we will become a less intrusive force in your economic decisions and daily life. Recent militancy in villages whose residents have had their land seized for use in public works projects by a supposedly less intrusive state may rhyme with outbursts of rural violence of earlier decades or even centuries, as Chinese farmers have opposed the government many times. But such protests are not just like those of any earlier period. The context is different. So, too, are the technologies in play, which, for example, allow farmers to use cell phones to leak news of state violence to foreign journalists.

There are other ways in which even trying to find rhymes with the past may mislead us as we try to make sense of China in an era when it has continually defied the predictions of the savviest analysts, stubbornly refusing to get with what influential figures such as Francis Fukuyama have assured us is definitely the program for the new millennium. What are we to do if we are interested in sorting out the future prospects of a country that continues to be governed by a Communist Party, albeit one that has admitted capitalists in its ranks, more than a decade and a half after the "Leninist extinction" was pronounced? Maybe a first step is to acknowledge that, for the moment at least, while we might learn interesting things by listening for and teasing out hidden rhyme schemes, China's present has unfolded in what are basically unexpected ways. And we should remember, as a cautionary tale, that someone focusing only on rhymes when listening to a poet perform will end up looking foolish if the artist turns out to have been presenting the audience with a piece of free verse.

Acknowledgments

Even though this is a short book, it developed over a long stretch of time, leaving me with many people to thank. I want to begin with the two groups to whom the work is dedicated. First, closest to home, Anne Bock, Sam Bock, and Gina Bock, who accompanied me on several of the trips described above and always made me happy to return from the ones I took on my own. Individually, I want to thank Anne for working hard to earn us accommodation in a "Foreign Experts" apartment during our 1986/87 sojourn in Shanghai (a debt I'll never quite be able to repay, though I keep trying); Sam for giving me a valuable and always candid teenage perspective on what was most and least interesting about the tales I had to tell about my trips; and Gina for letting me benefit from her budding photographic skills (and putting up with my needing to be on the road on some of her May 4th birthdays).

Second, I want to thank the many newspaper, magazine, and journal editors with whom I have worked since the mid-1990s when I began to make serious efforts to regularly publish my ideas in periodicals aimed at general audiences. Among these, Alan Jenkins deserves special mention: four of the chapters in the book began as contributions to the "Letters from . . ." *Times Literary Supplement* series he ran so skillfully. Many other editors taught me important things, in some cases by working with me on individual pieces that evolved into chapters, in other cases simply by helping me in other ways with what I have come to see as a decade-long (and still unfinished) post-tenure apprenticeship in the craft of public writing. (Some even assisted me by telling me in detail what they thought worked best and least well about a submission that they did not accept for publication.) In particular, I want to thank Nayan Chanda, Deb Chasman, Sandy Close, Joshua Cohen, Will Dobson, Holly Eley, Anne Fadiman, Jeanne Ferris, Bill Finan, Susan Greenberg, Nisid Hajari, Jane Kamensky, Steve Lagerfeld, Paul Laity, Hugh Lamberton, Kate Palmer, Hugo Restall, Michael Walzer, Natasha Wimmer, Art Winslow, and Linda Wrigley.

I also owe debts of gratitude to three other groups of people: friends, relatives, and colleagues who read and commented on chapters, or listened to and commented on oral versions of tales that later became chapters; people who encouraged or supported in varied ways my turn toward public writing; and the many individuals who shared their ideas about China and other places with me while I was on the road. I can't hope to mention everyone in these groups who deserves thanks, but I'd be remiss not to make an effort to single some people out.

In terms of readers (and listeners), I am grateful to many of my former Indiana University colleagues, including John Bodnar, Purnima Bose, Moureen Coulter, Jeff Gould, Mike Grossberg, Jeff Isaac, Tom Keirstead, Scott Kennedy, Deidre Lynch, Scott O'Bryan, Eric Sandweiss, Dror Wahrman, Jeff Veidlinger, and especially Maria Bucur, Nick Cullather, Tom Gieryn, and Ken Dau-Schmidt, who read or heard more than most; my parents (Phyllis and Richard Wasserstrom, who also deserve thanks for getting me hooked on international travel at a young age) and my parents-in-law (Fred and JoLynne Jones); and the following people scattered around the world, each of whom read and commented on more than one chapter: Geremie Barmé, Robert Bickers, Tim Cheek, Harriet Evans, John Fitzgerald, Lynn Hunt, Dan Letwin, Sheila Levine, Susan McEachern, Barbara Mittler, Vanessa Schwartz, Steve Smith, Julia Thomas, Michael Tsin, and Lindsay Waters. Above all, in this category, I am grateful to Yomi Braester, Michael Schudson, and Peter Zarrow (three colleagues who read complete manuscripts at the behest of Indiana University Press and revealed their identities after submitting their generous readers' reports) and Liz Perry and Paul

Cohen (two friends and mentors who, over the years, have read far more of my writings than I had any right to expect them, or indeed anyone, to read).

In terms of support for my turn toward public writing, I am grateful to Perry Anderson, Joyce Appleby, James Banner, Craig Calhoun, Carol Gluck, Merle Goldman, Harriet Evans, Orville Schell, Jonathan Spence, Kumble R. Subbaswamy, Frederic Wakeman, and Marilyn Young. I am also grateful to two Irvine colleagues, Ken Pomeranz and Steve Topik. Their book, *The World That Trade Created,* helped convince me that a volume like this was worth trying to write, and Steve encouraged me at a key moment not to give up on the idea.

When it comes to people who shared their ideas with me while I was on the road, I am especially grateful to John Gittings (for many things, not least the wonderful accommodations in the former French Concession in 2002) and to Lynn Pan, Yilin W., Liu Xinyong, Patricia Stranahan, and Iris Z. (each of whom gave me the benefit of his or her unique perspective on Shanghai). In addition, I want to thank Adam Brookes, David Kenley, Susan Lawrence, Barbara Mittler, and Steve Smith (for helping me understand the 1999 protests, and in David's case also letting me include one of the photos he took on May 9); Maria Csanadi, Miklos Haraszti, Gabriella Ivacs, and Istvan Rev (for their insights about Budapest); Joan Curts and Anne Prescott for including me as a guest lecturer on tours of China they led; Hsiung Ping-chen, Leng Tse-kang, Michael McGerr, and Peter Zarrow (for time spent together in Taipei); Jim, Maureen, Adrian and Emma McClure (for, among other things, introducing me to the "Feast of the Hunter's Moon"); and Woody and Rubie Watson (for hospitality and conversations in Cambridge, Mass.).

I also owe a very special thanks to Steve Raymer, Ivan Soros, and Alan Thomas for the wonderful photographs they let me use. And, last but far from least, I am grateful to Vladimir Tismaneanu, for generously making time to write the foreword to this volume, and Rebecca Tolen of Indiana University Press, who helped persuade me to do this book and then did so much to shape it as it developed from an idea into a manuscript. Needless to say, none of those thanked above should be held responsible in any way for the opinions expressed in this book.

Chapter 1 draws on material originally published in the author's "Burgers, Bowling, and the Myth of Americanizing China," *Dissent,* Fall 1998, 22–25, and is used here courtesy of that periodical.

Chapters 2, 8, 10, and 14 draw on material originally published in the *Times Literary Supplement* (London) in the issues dated January 3, 2003; December 31, 1999; July 28, 2000; and November 16, 2001. The author is grateful to the *TLS* for permission to republish this material here.

Chapter 3 contains some material that first appeared in "A Tide of Civic Pride," *Newsweek* (International Editions), October 7, 2002, and is republished here courtesy of that periodical.

Chapter 5 is adapted from "Searching for Emily Hahn on the Streets of St. Louis," which appeared in the spring 2006 issue of *History Workshop Journal* and is republished here courtesy of Oxford University Press.

Chapter 6 contains some abridged material from the author's "Traveling with Twain in an Age of Simulations," which first appeared in the April 2004 issue of *Common-Place,* and appears here courtesy of that periodical.

Chapter 11 contains material that first appeared in "Flagging Standards: Patriotism in Public Life," *Australian Financial Review: Weekend Review Magazine,* November 16, 2001, and is used here courtesy of the *AFR.*

Chapter 13 contains material that first appeared in the September 2003 issue of *Current History,* in an essay titled "China's Brave New World," and is used here courtesy of that periodical.

Bibliography of Works Discussed

Abbas, Akbar. "Play It Again Shanghai: Urban Preservation in the Global Era." In *Shanghai Reflections: Architecture, Urbanism, and the Search for an Alternative Modernity,* edited by Mario Gandelsona, 37–55. Princeton, N.J.: Princeton Architectural Press, 2002.

Barmé, Geremie R. "The Garden of Perfect Brightness: A Life in Ruins." *East Asian History* 11 (June 1996): 111–158.

Baudrillard, Jean. *Simulations.* New York: Semiotext(e), 1983.

Bedford, Sybille. *Aldous Huxley: A Biography.* New York: Knopf, 1974.

Bennett, Tony. "The Exhibitionary Complex." *New Formations* 4 (1988): 73–103.

Bernstein, Richard and Ross H. Munro. *The Coming Conflict with China.* New York: Knopf, 1997.

Buck, Pearl S. *The Good Earth.* New York: John Day, 1931.

Buruma, Ian. "Asia World." *New York Review of Books,* June 12, 2003, 54–57.

Chang, Jung and Jon Halliday. *Mao: The Unknown Story.* New York: Knopf, 2005.

Cook, Thomas. *Letters from the Sea and from Foreign Lands: Descriptive of a Tour Round the World.* 1873. Reprint, London: Routledge, 1998.

Crick, Bernard. *George Orwell: A Life.* Boston: Little, Brown, 1980.

Cuoco, Lorin and William H. Gass, eds. *Literary St. Louis: A Guide.* St. Louis: Missouri Historical Society Press, 2000.

Davis, Susan G. *Spectacular Nature: Corporate Culture and the Sea World Experience.* Berkeley: University of California Press, 1997.

Drakulić, Slavenka. *Café Europa: Life After Communism.* New York: Norton, 1997.

————. *How We Survived Communism and Even Laughed.* New York: HarperPerennial, 1993.

Eco, Umberto. *Travels in Hyperreality: Essays.* Translated by William Weaver from the Italian. San Diego: Harcourt Brace Jovanovich, 1990.

Friedman, Thomas L. *The World is Flat: A Brief History of the Twenty-First Century.* New York: Farrer, Straus, Giroux, 2005.

Hahn, Emily. *The Soong Sisters.* New York: Doubleday, 1943.

————. *China to Me: A Partial Autobiography.* New York: Doubleday, 1945.

————. *England to Me.* New York: Doubleday, 1949.

————. *Africa to Me: Person to Person.* New York: Doubleday, 1964.

————. *Times and Places: A Memoir.* New York: Thomas Y. Crowell and Co., 1970.

Harris, Neil, et al., eds. *Grand Illusions: Chicago's World's Fair of 1893.* Chicago: Chicago Historical Society, 1993.

Harvey, David. *Spaces of Capital: Towards a Critical Geography.* New York: Routledge, 2001.

Henry, Joel and Rachel Antony, *The Lonely Planet Guide to Experimental Travel.* London and Oakland, Calif.: Lonely Planet Publications, 2005.

Huxley, Aldous, *Brave New World.* New York: HarperPerennial Modern Classics Reprint Edition, 1998.

————. *The Doors of Perception.* New York: Perennial, 1970.

Isaacs, Harold R. *Scratches on Our Minds: American Views of China and India.* New York: John Day Co., 1958.

James, Henry. *The Aspern Papers and Other Stories.* New York: Penguin, 1976.

Kristof, Nicholas and Sheryl WuDunn. *China Wakes: The Struggle for the Soul of a Rising Power.* New York: Times Books, 1994.

Kuan, Seng and Peter G. Rowe, eds. *Shanghai: Architecture & Urbanism for Modern China.* New York: Prestel, 2004.

Li, Gui. *Huan you diqiu xin lu* [A New Account of a Trip Around the Globe]. Shanghai: n.p., 1878.

————. *A Journey to the East: Li Gui's* A New Account of a Trip Around the Globe. Translated and with an introduction by Charles Desnoyers. Ann Arbor: University of Michigan Press, 2004.

Lim, William. *Have You Been Shanghaied?* Singapore: Asian Urban Lab, 2004.

McCabe, James D. *The Illustrated History of the Centennial Exhibition.* 1876. Reprint, Philadelphia, Pa. National Publishing Company, 1975.

Meyers, Jeffrey. *Orwell: Wintry Conscience of a Generation.* New York: Norton, 2000.

Orwell, George. *1984: A Novel.* 1949. Reprint, New York: New American Library, 1989.

Paloczi-Horvath, George. *Mao Tse-Tung: Emperor of the Blue Ants.* London: Secker and Werburg, 1962.

Salisbury, Harrison E. *The New Emperors: China in the Era of Mao and Deng.* Boston: Little, Brown, 1992.

Sandweiss, Lee Ann. *Seeking St. Louis: Voices from a River City, 1670–2000.* St. Louis: Missouri Historical Society Press, 2000.

Schwartz, Vanessa R. *Spectacular Realities: Early Mass Culture in Fin-de-Siècle Paris.* Berkeley: University of California Press, 1998.

Sorkin, Michael, ed. *Variations on a Theme Park: The New American City and the End of Public Space.* New York: Hill and Wang, 1992.

Stephenson, Neal. *The Diamond Age: Or, a Young Lady's Illustrated Primer.* New York: Bantam, 1995.

Stilgoe, John R. *Outside Lies Magic: Regaining History and Awareness in Everyday Places.* New York: Walker and Company, 1998.

Twain, Mark. *The Innocents Abroad or The New Pilgrims' Progress.* 1869. Reprint, New York: Bantam, 1964.

———. *Roughing It.* 1872. Reprint, Oxford: Oxford University Press, 1996.

Verne, Jules. *Around the World in Eighty Days.* 1873. Reprint, translated by George M. Towle with an introduction by Bruce Sterling, New York: Modern Library, 2003.

———. *The Tribulations of a Chinaman in China.* 1880. Reprint, Amsterdam: Fredonia Books, 2001.

Wakeman, Frederic E., Jr. "Revolutionary Rites: The Remains of Chiang Kai-shek and Mao Tse-tung." *Representations* 10 (Spring 1985): 146–93.

Watson, James L., ed. *Golden Arches East: McDonald's in East Asia.* Stanford, Calif.: Stanford University Press, 1997, second edition 2006.

Young, John Russell. *Around the World with General Grant.* 1879. Reprint, edited, abridged, and introduced by Michael Fellman, Baltimore, Md.: The Johns Hopkins University Press, 2002.

Zoujin shibohui [Entering the World Expo]. Shanghai, 2002.

Index

Italicized page numbers indicate illustrations.

Jeffrey N. Wasserstrom is Professor of History at the University of California, Irvine. He specializes in the study of modern and contemporary China and in comparative cultural history. His books include *Student Protests in Twentieth-Century China: The View from Shanghai* and the co-edited volumes *Human Rights and Revolutions* and *Chinese Femininities/Chinese Masculinities.* He served as a core consultant for Carma Hinton and Richard Gordon's *The Gate of Heavenly Peace,* an acclaimed documentary film on the Tiananmen upheaval of 1989.